CYPRUS

DIVIDED ISLAND

CYPRUS
DIVIDED ISLAND

by Tom Streissguth

Lerner Publications Company / Minneapolis

Website address: www.lernerbooks.com

All maps by Philip Schwartzberg, Meridian Mapping, Minneapolis.
Cover photo © Gino Russo.
Table of contents photos (from top to bottom) by Archive Photos/Reuters/Costa Kyriakides; The London Illustrated News; Embassy of the Republic of Cyprus; Turkish Republic of Northern Cyprus; Institute for Multi-Track Diplomacy.

Series Consultant: Andrew Bell-Fialkoff
Editor: Cynthia Harris
Editorial Director: Mary M. Rodgers
Designer: Michael Tacheny
Photo Researcher: Beth Osthoff

LIBRARY OF CONGRESS CATALOGING-IN-PUBLICATION DATA

Streissguth, Thomas, 1958–
Cyprus : divided island / by Tom Streissguth.
p. cm. — (World in conflict)
Includes bibliographical references and index.
Summary: A historical account of the ethnic conflict between Greek and Turkish factions on the island nation of Cyprus, including a discussion of current issues and challenges.
ISBN 0-8225-3551-3 (lib. bdg. : alk. paper)
1. Cyprus—Ethnic relations—Juvenile literature. [1. Cyprus. 2. Cyprus—Ethnic relations.] I. Title. II. Series.
DS54.5.S77 1998 96-26862
327.5645—DC20

Manufactured in the United States of America
1 2 3 4 5 6 - JR - 03 02 01 00 99 98

CONTENTS

ABOUT THIS SERIES

Government firepower kills 25 protesters . . . . Thousands of refugees flee the country . . . . Rebels attack capital . . . . Racism and rage flare . . . . Fighting breaks out . . . . Peace talks stall . . . . Bombing toll rises to 52 . . . . Slaughter has cost up to 50,000 lives.

Conflicts between people occur across the globe, and we hear about some of the more spectacular and horrific episodes in the news. But since most fighting doesn't directly affect us, we often choose to ignore it. And even if we do take the time to learn about these conflicts—from newspapers, magazines, television news, or radio—we're often left with just a snapshot of the conflict instead of the whole reel of film.

Most news accounts don't tell you the whole story about a conflict, focusing instead on the attention-grabbing events that make the headlines. In addition, news sources may have a preconceived idea about who is right and who is wrong in a conflict. The stories that result often portray one side as the "bad guys" and the other as the "good guys."

The *World in Conflict* series approaches each conflict with the idea that wars and political disputes aren't simply about bullies and victims. Conflicts are complex problems that can often be traced back hundreds of years. The people fighting one another have complicated reasons for doing so. Fighting erupts between groups divided by ethnicity, religion, and nationalism. These groups fight over power, money, territory, control. Sometimes people who just want to go about their own business get caught up in a conflict just because they're there.

These books examine major conflicts around the world, some of which are very bloody and others that haven't involved a lot of violence. They portray the people involved in and affected by conflicts. They describe how each conflict got started, how it developed, and where it stands. The books also outline some of the ways people have tried to end the conflicts. By reading the stories behind the headlines, you will learn some reasons why people hate and fight one another and, in addition, why some people struggle so hard to end conflicts.

WORDS YOU NEED TO KNOW

accession: The process by which one nation enters into an agreement already in force among other states.

Communist: A person who supports Communism—an economic system in which the government owns the means of producing goods in factories and of growing food.

coup d'état: French words meaning "blow to the state" that refer to a swift, sudden overthrow of a government.

enclave: An area or group that is culturally distinct from its surroundings, whether or not the area or group is enclosed within a foreign country.

ethnic background: A combination of cultural markers that bind a people into a distinctive, permanent group. These markers may include—but are not limited to—race, nationality, tribe, religion, language, customs, and historical origins.

federation: A form of government in which states or groups unite under a central power. The states or groups surrender individual sovereignty to make certain decisions but retain limited control over other aspects of government.

guerrilla: A rebel fighter, usually not associated with an internationally recognized government, who engages in irregular warfare. Membership in a guerrilla group usually indicates radical, aggressive, and unconventional activities.

intercommunal: Interaction between communities.

nationalism: A feeling of loyalty or patriotism toward one's nation, with a primary emphasis on the promotion of a national culture and national interests.

paramilitary: Describing a supplementary fighting force. Often, but not always, this term is used to describe underground, illegal groups. Sometimes an illegal paramilitary group may support, through the use of violence, the current government and its policies. The aim of other paramilitary groups is the overthrow of the government.

propaganda: Ideas, rumor, or information spread to influence people's opinion. The intent of propaganda may be either to injure or to promote an institution, a cause, or a people.

self-determination: The free choice, without external compulsion, of a people within a territorial unit to decide their own future political status.

FOREWORD

by Andrew Bell-Fialkoff

Conflicts between various groups are as old as time. Peoples and tribes around the world have fought one another for thousands of years. In fact our history is in great part a succession of wars—between the Greeks and the Persians, the English and the French, the Russians and the Poles, and many others. Not only do states or ethnic groups fight one another, so do followers of different religions—Catholics and Protestants in Northern Ireland, Christians and Muslims in Bosnia, and Buddhists and Hindus in Sri Lanka. Often ethnicity, language, and religion—some of the main distinguishing elements of culture—reinforce one another in characterizing a particular group. For instance, the vast majority of Greeks are Orthodox Christian and speak Greek; most Italians are Roman Catholic and speak Italian. Elsewhere, one cultural aspect predominates. Serbs and Croats speak dialects of the same language but remain separate from one another because most Croats are Catholics and most Serbs are Orthodox Christians. To those two groups, religion is more important than language in defining culture.

We have witnessed an increasing number of conflicts in modern times—why? Three reasons stand out. One is that large empires—such as Austria-Hungary, Ottoman Turkey, several colonial empires with vast holdings in Asia, Africa, and America, and, most recently, the Soviet Union—have collapsed. A look at world maps from 1900, 1950, and 1998 reveals an ever-increasing number of small and medium-sized states. While empires existed, their rulers suppressed many ethnic and religious conflicts. Empires imposed order, and local resentments were mostly directed at the central authority. Inside the borders of empires, populations were multiethnic and often highly mixed. When the empires fell apart, world leaders found it impossible to establish political frontiers that coincided with ethnic boundaries. Different groups often claimed territories inhabited by others. The nations created on the lands of a toppled empire were saddled with acute border and ethnic problems from their very beginnings.

The second reason for more conflicts in modern times stems from the twin ideals of freedom and equality. In the United States, we usually think of freedom as "individual freedom." If we all have equal rights, we are free. But if you are a member of a minority group and feel that you are being discriminated against, your group's rights and freedoms are also important to you. In fact, if you don't have your "group freedom," you don't have full individual freedom either.

After World War I (1914–1918), the allied western nations, under the guidance of U.S. president Woodrow Wilson, tried to satisfy group rights by promoting minority rights. The spread of frantic nationalism in the 1930s, especially among disaffected ethnic minorities, and the catastrophe of World War II (1939–1945) led to a fundamental reassessment of the Wilsonian philosophy. After 1945 group rights were downplayed on the assumption that guaranteeing individual rights would be sufficient. In later decades, the collapse of multiethnic nations like Czechoslovakia, Yugoslavia, and the Soviet Union—coupled with the spread of nationalism in those regions—came as a shock to world leaders. People want democracy and individual rights, but they want their group rights, too. In practice, this means more conflicts and a cycle of secession, as minority ethnic groups seek their own sovereignty and independence.

The fires of conflict are often further stoked by the media, which lavishes glory and attention on independence movements. To fight for freedom is an honor. For every Palestinian who has killed an Israeli, there are hundreds of Kashmiris, Tamils, and Bosnians eager to shoot at their enemies. Newspapers, television and radio news broadcasts, and other media play a vital part in fomenting that sense of honor. They magnify each crisis, glorify rebellion, and help to feed the fire of conflict.

The third factor behind increasing conflict in the world is the social and geographic mobility that modern society enjoys. We can move anywhere we want and can aspire—or so we believe—to be anything we wish. Every day the television tantalizingly dangles the prizes that life can offer. We all want our share. But increased mobility and ambition also mean increased competition, which leads to antagonism. Antagonism often fastens itself to ethnic, racial, or religious differences. If you are an inner-city African American and your local grocer happens to be Korean American, you may see that individual as different from yourself—an intruder—rather than as a person, a neighbor, or a grocer. This same feeling of "us" versus "them" has been part of many an ethnic conflict around the world.

Many conflicts have been contained—even solved—by wise, responsible leadership. But unfortunately, many politicians use citizens' discontent for their own ends. They incite hatred, manipulate voters, and mobilize people against their neighbors. The worst things happen when neighbor turns against neighbor. In Bosnia, in Rwanda, in Lebanon, and in countless other places, people who had lived and worked together and had even intermarried went on a rampage, killing, raping, and robbing one another with gusto. If the appalling carnage teaches us anything, it is that we should stop seeing one another as hostile competitors and enemies and accept one another as people. Most importantly, we should learn to understand why conflicts happen and how they can be prevented. That is why *World in Conflict* is so important—the books in this series will help you understand the history and inner dynamics of some of the most persistent conflicts of modern times. And understanding is the first step to prevention. 🌐

INTRODUCTION

Cyprus, the third-largest island in the Mediterranean Sea, sits 40 miles from the southern coast of Turkey and approximately 600 miles east of Greece. Directly south of Cyprus lies Egypt, on the North African coast. Cyprus is situated off the western coast of the Middle Eastern countries of Syria, Lebanon, and Israel.

International attention has become focused on the ethnically divided island, which is one of the most heavily militarized areas in the world. Almost all of the island's residents, called Cypriots, have either Greek or Turkish **ethnic backgrounds.** Since the late 1950s, tension between Greek Cypriots and Turkish Cypriots has periodically erupted into violent battles throughout the island. A shaky cease-fire and a heavily guarded buffer zone keep the ethnic communities apart, but war is not out of the question because neither side appears willing to compromise enough to resolve the conflict.

HOMELANDS

Cypriot government leaders and leaders of several other nations as well as nongovernmental organizations, such as the United Nations (UN), have attempted to bring peace to Cyprus, but no solution has been reached. Complicating the situation are feelings of **nationalism.** Most Cypriots feel more devoted to the culture and history of Greece or Turkey—the countries Cypriots consider their ancestral homelands—than they do to that of Cyprus. Ties of cultural heritage are more meaningful to many Cypriots than is the bond of geographic nearness.

Greece and Turkey, which share a border, have a history of competing for territory. Control of some lands has shifted between Turkey and Greece, resulting in the slaughter or expulsion of the population inhabiting the conquered region. In recent years, the countries have come to the brink of war several times.

Facing page: *Located in the eastern Mediterranean Sea, Cyprus covers about 3,600 square miles. At its longest point, the island spans 75 miles and is 128 miles across at its widest spot.*

MEDITERRANEAN SEA
Karpas Peninsula
Kyrenia / Girne
Kyrenia Mountains
TURKISH REPUBLIC
OF NORTHERN CYPRUS
Morphou Bay
Cape Kokkina
Morphou Plain
Khrysokhou Bay
Vouni
Soli
Attila Line
NICOSIA / LEFKOŞA
Mesaoria Plain
Famagusta Bay
Famagusta / Gazimagŭsa
Varosha
Dherinia
Attila Line
Dhekelia Base
REPUBLIC OF CYPRUS
Troodos Mountains
Larnaca Bay
Kitium
Larnaca
Paphos
Limassol
Kourion
Akrotiri Base
Akrotiri Bay
Episkopi Bay
0 10 20 30 40 50 miles
0 20 40 60 kilometers
NICOSIA / LEFKOŞA Capital
Famagusta Major City
Varosha Minor City
Kitium Historical site
Disputed boundary
Boundary of British military base
over 4,000 feet
2,000 feet
1,000 feet
500 feet
250 feet
sea level

Besides territorial issues, Greece and Turkey have clashed over rights in the Aegean Sea, over military airspace, and over membership in the European Union (EU), an alliance of many European countries. Greece is an EU member. Turkey has a customs union with the EU and is applying for full membership—a move that Greek representatives have vetoed.

Nationalism has often motivated Greece and Turkey to influence the Cyprus conflict. In 1974 both nations took military action on the island on behalf of their ethnic kin. That intervention and prejudices stemming from the past and present hatred between the homelands play a role in shaping Cypriots' attitudes and the relations between Cyprus's ethnic communities.

Cultural and Tourism Office of the Turkish Embassy

Dating from the sixteenth century, this miniature (small painting) shows the enthroned Ottoman sultan (ruler) accepting the bow of a visiting prince. The Ottoman Turks governed Cyprus for three centuries. During this period, many Turkish-speakers emigrated from Turkey, creating a new society of Turkish-speaking Cypriots.

PATH TO SEGREGATION

Greek Cypriots and Turkish Cypriots shared the island in relative peace for nearly four centuries. For most of that time, the island was under external rule. Turkey governed Cyprus for close to 300 years and then Britain for about 100 more.

Beginning in the nineteenth century, many Greek Cypriots pressed for the end of British rule and for union with Greece. As the years passed, Greek Cypriots increased their pressure on Britain. Turkish Cypriots did not want to live under Greek rule. When it seemed likely that Britain was going to give in to pressure from Greek Cypriots, Turkish Cypriots advocated partitioning the island into ethnic zones and allowing each zone to unite with its respective homeland.

Britain granted the island its independence in 1960. Independence did not come without restrictions, however. Britain, Greece, and Turkey were called upon to help Cypriots develop the new republic's constitution. The resulting document prohibited either union with Greece or partition. But Greek Cypriots' strong desire to unite with Greece did not diminish, and **intercommunal** violence broke out when they continued to press for union.

Archive Photos/Express Newspapers

Cyprus achieved independence from Britain on August 16, 1960, when the retiring governor Sir Hugh Foot (center) *handed power to President Makarios* (left) *and Vice President Küçük* (right).

The segregation of Greek Cypriots and Turkish Cypriots took place in two stages. In the early 1960s, Turkish Cypriots clustered together in ethnic **enclaves** throughout the island. During the summer of 1974, severe fighting in Cyprus, in which both Turkey and Greece were also involved, finalized the island's division into two distinct ethnic zones. Turkish Cypriots fled to northern Cyprus; Greek Cypriots to southern Cyprus. Since that time, almost all Cypriots have remained segregated by ethnicity.

A buffer zone called the Attila Line prevents Greek Cypriots or Turkish Cypriots from freely crossing to the other ethnic community's zone. The UN supports a small network of peacekeepers and watchtowers to regulate the passage of individuals across the buffer zone. UN troops also keep apart the military forces of the north and south, which are stationed along cease-fire lines on either side of the buffer zone.

The Attila Line

Dividing the Republic of Cyprus and the Turkish Republic of Northern Cyprus (TRNC) is the Attila Line, a 112-mile-long buffer zone that zigzags west to east from Morphou Bay to Famagusta Bay. The UN established the zone in 1974 to separate the territories and to keep apart Greek Cypriot and Turkish troops. The Attila Line means something very different to Greek Cypriots and Turkish Cypriots. For Turkish Cypriots, the buffer zone is a national sovereign border. Greek Cypriots view it as a boundary between occupied Cyprus and the free, government-controlled portion of the island.

Most of the line runs through rural areas, where two parallel barbed-wire fences mark the buffer zone. In some places, the buffer zone is over four miles wide. From UN watchtowers, peacekeepers constantly observe the land between the fences. There is activity just beyond the fences, too, where Greek Cypriot troops keep lookout on one side and Turkish troops patrol the other.

In Nicosia the Attila Line divides the city into Greek Cypriot and Turkish Cypriot sectors. (The current line splits the capital along the same path as an earlier barrier, called the Green Line, which the British established in 1964.) Parts of Nicosia's buffer zone consist of stacked oil drums and concrete barriers, and in the capital it's much narrower than it is in the countryside. In some places, less than 70 feet separate the cease-fire lines. On Hermes Street, for example, one side of the road is Turkish Cypriot territory and the other is Greek Cypriot.

In Nicosia, the divided capital of Cyprus, oil drums mark a portion of the Attila Line, which was established in 1974 to separate the island's two warring ethnic communities.

Houses and shops along the line have been boarded up, and the neighborhoods are deserted. Soldiers from forces in either Cypriot territory need to walk only a few paces in the wrong direction to violate the cease-fire.

From watchtowers United Nations peacekeeping forces monitor the buffer zone between Turkish Cypriot and Greek Cypriot areas.

Both governments restrict travel across the Attila Line, and they maintain checkpoints to regulate passage. For the most part, the TRNC gives permission sparingly to Turkish Cypriots who want to travel to the Republic of Cyprus. After receiving permission from the TRNC government, the small number of Greek Cypriots who still live in the north can travel to the Republic of Cyprus for several days each month. A new regulation in the TRNC allows the children of northern Greek Cypriots who attend school in the south to return to the TRNC on weekends and holidays without filing for permission each time. Greek Cypriots living in the south may apply to the TRNC for permission to visit relatives in the north for one day each month. But many Greek Cypriots won't cross the Attila Line. Some feel that doing so and signing Turkish Cypriot documents would mean they acknowledged the authority of the TRNC over northern Cyprus. Others fear they would be harassed—physically or economically—by fellow Republic of Cyprus citizens.

Laws in the Republic of Cyprus permit Greek Cypriots and foreign tourists to go north during the day, but they cannot spend the night. The Republic of Cyprus also asks travelers not to purchase goods in the TRNC. Greek Cypriot officials don't want tourists to support the economy of the unrecognized government of northern Cyprus. If a tourist tries to reenter the Republic of Cyprus with TRNC merchandise, the goods may be confiscated at the checkpoint. Turkish Cypriots living in the south can also travel to the TRNC. In an exception to the law that travelers must return by sundown, the Republic of Cyprus allows its Turkish Cypriot citizens to stay in northern Cyprus as long as they like, provided they are staying with relatives or friends and are not contributing to the TRNC economy by patronizing a hotel. But depending on the political climate, the governments sometimes completely ban travel across the Attila Line. In these cases, families with relatives on both sides of the line may leave Cyprus and meet in a different country so they can avoid the travel restrictions at home.

ONE GOVERNMENT OR TWO?

By 1983, when no progress toward an overall settlement had been reached, Turkish Cypriots declared independence. They named northern Cyprus, the 37 percent of the island under their control, the Turkish Republic of Northern Cyprus (TRNC).

For the sake of clarity, in this book the term the Republic of Cyprus refers to the area of Cyprus (south of the Attila Line) that is under Greek Cypriot control. The land north of the buffer zone, where the Turkish Cypriot community lives, will be called the TRNC.

SCENIC CYPRUS

Beyond the guns, tanks, and barbed wire, Cyprus is a scenic island. Tourist resorts take advantage of the island's extensive shoreline. Two mountain ranges dominate its landscape. The Kyrenia Mountains, in northern Cyprus, reach about 3,000 feet in elevation. These steep limestone highlands extend into the Karpas Peninsula, a long, narrow finger of land that points northeastward to the coasts of Turkey and Syria. The Troodos Mountains cover most of southern Cyprus. Fruit orchards and vineyards grow on its foothills, while forests of oak and pine thrive at higher altitudes.

Between the two mountain ranges lies the flat and fertile Mesaoria Plain, the breadbasket of Cyprus, which stretches from the Morphou Plain in the west to Famagusta Bay in the east. The Attila Line runs through the Mesaoria Plain, most of which falls in Turkish Cypriot territory.

The island's capital city straddles the buffer zone and is divided into Greek Cypriot and Turkish Cypriot quarters. Nicosia (population 233,318) is the Greek Cypriot name for the city and the name used by most of the world. Turkish Cypriots call the capital Lefkoşa.

Limassol, with a population of 148,700, and Larnaca (population 66,400) are the largest ports in the Republic of Cyprus. Famagusta, called Gazimagũsa by Turkish

What's in a Name?

Each ethnic community resents how the other group's government refers to itself. Turkish Cypriot leaders claim that Greek Cypriot officials should not call themselves the government of the Republic of Cyprus because that was the name given to the country when the ethnic communities shared joint rule. They blame Greek and Greek Cypriot actions for causing Turkey's military involvement and the division of the communities into ethnic zones under separate governments. By using the name the Republic of Cyprus, TRNC officials complain, Greek Cypriots give the false impression of being the legitimate government of all Cypriot people.

Neither the Greek Cypriot-controlled government of southern Cyprus nor the rest of the world—with the exception of Turkey—recognizes the TRNC as a legal political entity. Many Greek Cypriots view the government in the south, run entirely by Greek Cypriots, as the island's only government. The government of the Republic of Cyprus perceives the island's division to be a consequence of Turkey's 1974 military intervention, which Greek Cypriot leaders label an illegal invasion.

Tourists enjoy visiting Cyprus's many historic buildings. This Roman temple, dating to the first century A.D.*, stands near the ancient ruins of Kourion in the southern part of the island.*

Cypriots, has 21,983 people. It and Kyrenia (population 7,810), also called Girne, are the major ports in the TRNC.

CULTURES OF CYPRUS

Turkish Cypriot officials have not allowed an official census of their community since the 1960s, when intercommunal clashes intensified. Because the relative populations of the ethnic communities may have a significant impact on an overall political settlement, each Cypriot government questions the accuracy of the numbers reported by the other. A widely reported estimate claims that the population in Cyprus in the mid-1990s numbered almost 815,000. Greek Cypriots made up slightly more than 78 percent of that figure, while Turkish Cypriots and the many Turks who moved to Cyprus after 1974 accounted for about 20 percent. People of British descent make up most of the remaining population. In addition to the permanent residents, 3,900 British soldiers are stationed on the island.

Both Greek Cypriots and Turkish Cypriots have lived in Cyprus since the late 1500s. Cultural, religious, and language differences prevented intermarriage and the emergence of a people with a single national identity. Almost all Turkish Cypriots are Muslims, or followers of the Islamic religion. The majority of Greek Cypriots are Orthodox Christians. Few Cypriots can speak or read both Greek and Turkish. Most understand only the language of their ethnic heritage, especially in the villages. If a Cypriot does know two languages, most likely the second language is English.

Negative cultural stereotypes play a role in perpetuating the disdain many

Cypriots feel for those of the other ethnicity. Greek Cypriots are said to be pushy and wily, whereas Turkish Cypriots are called lazy and stupid. These unattractive characterizations make their way into the mainstream media, and even into government publications, coloring Cypriots' impression of those from the "other side."

© Andrew E. Beswick

Fruit pickers load oranges into baskets. The 1974 fighting forced many farmers to leave their land. Turkish Cypriot leaders—after claiming that Greek Cypriots abandoned their holdings in northern Cyprus—permitted Turkish settlers or Turkish Cypriots to farm there. Still unresolved, the settlement question is a bone of contention between the ethnic communities.

THE ECONOMIES OF CYPRUS

In the mid-twentieth century, Cyprus experienced strong economic growth. The development of new industries in cities, new irrigation projects in the countryside, and a busy tourism sector provided Cypriots with good jobs. Beginning in the 1960s—due to discord between the communities—Turkish Cypriots came to depend heavily on Turkey for their economic survival.

The Greek Cypriot community continued to flourish for another decade, but intercommunal violence and the island's division in 1974 also squelched the Greek Cypriot economy. In the 1970s, Greek Cypriots saw trade with other countries cease, saw tourism slow, and saw unemployment rise to nearly 30 percent.

The prolonged division of Cyprus has fractured the island's economy. The Republic of Cyprus—aided by the international recognition of its government—recovered quickly, and these days its citizens enjoy almost full employment. Financial aid received by the Republic of Cyprus from international organizations—such as the EU, to which the Republic of Cyprus desires to belong—has been invested in projects that benefit the southern, Greek Cypriot population. The Republic of Cyprus's government has given tax breaks and other incentives to encourage growth. The government has also invested in new factories, ports, and roads and has renewed trade with Europe and the Middle East. By the early 1990s, southern Cyprus had rebuilt its industries and had achieved stable economic growth.

A lack of trade and outside investment has hurt the TRNC's economy. Few foreign businesses will deal with a region that has not received international recognition as a legal political entity. The Republic of Cyprus government has kept most goods and tourists, except those from Turkey, from arriving or leaving the TRNC by declaring it illegal for ships to dock at northern ports or for planes to fly into northern airports. According to Greek Cypriot leaders, the only way to enter the TRNC legally is through UN-controlled points of entry along the buffer zone.

Lack of capital has restricted the TRNC's efforts to modernize its economy. For instance, little investment has been made in manufacturing. After receiving education at foreign universities, many Turkish Cypriots choose to leave Cyprus permanently because the stagnant economy means that they cannot get good jobs. Unemployment is also high among Turkish Cypriots because they compete for jobs with continually growing numbers of Turkish peasants who have been encouraged to settle in Cyprus and are willing to work for low wages. Another factor that lowers Turkish Cypriots' standard of living is a high rate of inflation.

Although Turkish Cypriots have access to more farmland and natural resources than do Greek Cypriots, agriculture and mining have declined because, except for Turkey, the TRNC does not have trading partners. Until 1994 the TRNC managed to export a significant amount of citrus and other produce, two-thirds of which went to EU members. In that year—on the heels of a UN report criticizing the TRNC's "political unwillingness" to negotiate with the Republic of Cyprus—the EU's European Court of Justice ruled that its member-states could no longer import TRNC agricultural products. Agreement on that point, however, has not moved the two sides any closer to finding a solution that overcomes the major barriers between Greek Cypriots and Turkish Cypriots.

Turkish Republic of Northern Cyprus

Turkish vacationers walk along a street in Kyrenia (Girne), a large city in the territory of the Turkish Republic of Northern Cyprus (TRNC). Before Cyprus's division, tourism was an important part of the local economy. Since 1974, however, Turkey is the only country willing to land planes at northern Cyprus's airports or to dock ships in the area's ports.

DEADLOCK

For many years, the official platform of leaders from each ethnic community has been that the island should be reunited under one government. UN resolutions have also promoted the creation of a Cypriot **federation,** or two states drawn together under a central government.

Leaders in each community hold strong opinions about how Cyprus should be governed. Greek Cypriot politicans want a strong central government that regulates many aspects of island life. Turkish Cypriot leaders, on the other hand, want a weaker central government that leaves each community free to control certain issues of concern.

Although both governments in Cyprus have said they want to live under a central government, distrust between community leaders is high. As a result, each side also has made backup plans with its homeland to ensure survival in case the Cypriot communities do not reach agreement. Turkey continues to provide security in the TRNC and has promised to do so until the Turkish Cypriots' status in Cyprus is guaranteed in an overall settlement. Meanwhile, the Republic of Cyprus maintains its relations with Greece. In November 1993, Greece and the Republic of Cyprus signed a mutual defense agreement that Greece guarantees military protection to the Greek Cypriots.

Turkish Republic of Northern Cyprus

A Turkish Cypriot villager bakes bread in an outdoor brick oven. Many of the modernizations that have occurred in southern Cyprus have yet to reach the TRNC, where the income per person is less than one-fourth of the average income of people in the Republic of Cyprus.

THE EU ISSUE

In the mid-1990s, Turkish Cypriots had a per capita income of less than $3,100, while on average Greek Cypriots earned $13,650. Some Turkish Cypriots call the Republic of Cyprus's embargo on Turkish Cypriot goods a form of economic warfare. Rather than increasing the chance of settlement, the embargo, Turkish Cypriots say, encourages tighter ties between the TRNC and Turkey, its sole economic supporter. Greek Cypriots, on the other hand, resent that those living in the TRNC, who make up about 20 percent of Cyprus's population, hold 37 percent of the island, including much of its fertile cropland and mineral resources.

Although Greek Cypriots have fared better economically than have Turkish Cypriots, the conflict has disrupted both economies. With the island's strategic location, all its residents would greatly benefit from full-scale foreign trade and investment. In addition, a settlement would remove the need to spend a tremendous amount on military preparations.

The hope of the Republic of Cyprus to become a full EU member could draw together southern and northern Cyprus or could wedge them even further apart. Both sides realize that EU membership would bring large economic benefits. Cyprus would be able to export more manufactured and agricultural goods. Production of these goods would increase, allowing Cypriots better wages and a higher standard of living.

But EU membership before a federal settlement, TRNC leaders believe, would leave no incentive for Greek Cypriots to return to the negotiating table. If only southern Cyprus were a member, only Greek Cypriots would receive the economic benefits. The unrecognized TRNC would be further isolated, and an even greater gap in the standards of living between the ethnic zones would result.

In June 1994, the TRNC government threatened to formally join northern Cyprus to Turkey if the EU accepted the Republic of Cyprus as a member. The Republic of Cyprus government, meanwhile, does not believe its economic health should be tied to its negotiations with the TRNC. The Republic of Cyprus seeks to move forward on the EU application, insisting that the TRNC accept the EU application as a precondition for southern Cyprus to resume talks.

As a result, the EU, which has its headquarters in Brussels, Belgium, has been drawn into the Cyprus conflict. Although the EU seeks to avoid ethnic and political strife among its members, the organization also wants to extend into the eastern Mediterranean. In the meantime, both Greek Cypriot and Turkish Cypriot leaders use EU membership as a bargaining chip.

A Greek Cypriot refugee reports, "When I come to work, . . . I can see a Turkish family from the mainland working just a stone's throw away, across the barbed wire [along the buffer zone], on what used to be our field."

In addition to the difficulties of creating a modern federation, Greek Cypriots and Turkish Cypriots must also face problems from the past. In the 1960s and 1970s, hundreds of thousands of Cypriots became refugees, losing their homes, land, and businesses. Any settlement between the two sides needs to resolve claims to lost property. Also of high priority is an accounting of individuals who have been listed as missing since the decades of intercommunal violence.

Extremist factions exist, and their goal is to perpetuate the division of Cyprus's population. But a growing number of Cypriots from each ethnic zone believe they must rebuild lines of trust for any solution to last. For these peacemaking groups and individuals, the increasing animosity between the governments of the Republic of Cyprus and the TRNC reveals the sizable challenges that lie ahead.

Embassy of the Republic of Cyprus

Glafkos Clerides

Turkish Republic of Northern Cyprus

Rauf Denktaş

EU Emblem

MAJOR PLAYERS IN THE CONFLICT

Clerides, Glafkos Elected president of the Republic of Cyprus in 1993. Beginning in 1968, he represented Greek Cypriots in intercommunal talks until 1976. That year he founded the Democratic Rally Party, which encourages a practical, intercommunal settlement.

Denktaş, Rauf Long-time Turkish Cypriot leader, he declared the sovereignty of the Turkish Republic of Northern Cyprus (TRNC) in 1983 and has held the presidency since then. In the late 1950s, Denktaş helped organize the Turkish Resistance Organization. He represented Turkish Cypriots in intercommunal talks that began in 1968. In 1975 Turkish Cypriots elected Denktaş president of the self-declared Turkish Federated State of Cyprus.

European Union (EU) Formerly known as the European Community—which was established to strengthen economic ties between its members—this organization requires its European member-countries to unite in many realms. By eliminating trade barriers, the association promotes members' economic cooperation. The EU took its current name in 1993, when its control expanded to include military matters, law enforcement, and immigration. People born in an EU member-country have European citizenship and can live and work anywhere in the union. Countries applying for EU membership must meet strict EU standards in economic and human rights practices.

Greece (Hellenic Republic) Has never ruled Cyprus, but many Greek Cypriots feel that Greece is their homeland. Greece and the Republic of Cyprus have cultural, political, and military bonds. The countries entered a common defense pact in 1993 and have agreed to make joint decisions regarding a Cyprus settlement. An EU member, Greece lobbies for the Republic of Cyprus's admission and has worked to block Turkey's application.

North Atlantic Treaty Organization (NATO) Formed in 1949 by European and North American countries to provide mutual defense against attacks by the Soviet Union or any other aggressor. Although both Greece and Turkey are NATO members, the historic enemies have threatened one another over Cyprus and other issues. In several instances, NATO has negotiated firmly to prevent these member-countries from going to war.

Turkey, Republic of Conquered Cyprus in 1571 and ruled it until 1878. Many Turkish Cypriots regard Turkey as their homeland. Since 1974, when Greece and Turkey took military action in Cyprus, Turkish troops have patrolled northern Cyprus, maintaining the island's division into ethnic zones, and thousands of mainland Turks have settled there. Turkey threatens to integrate the TRNC if the EU grants membership to the Republic of Cyprus and denies it to Turkey.

United Nations (UN) A nongovernmental agency set up in 1945 to work for world peace. In 1964 the UN sent peacekeeping troops to Cyprus after intercommunal fighting broke out. UN forces—under the acronym UNFICYP— still guard Cyprus's buffer zone.

Hellenic Republic

NATO Emblem

Republic of Turkey

CHAPTER 1

THE RECENT CONFLICT AND ITS EFFECTS

Even though Cypriots say that a settlement to the decades-long conflict would be in the best interest of everyone involved, the outlook for a solution seems farther away than ever. What most ordinary citizens want—a peaceful land where they can live in safety—escapes the efforts of politicians and peacemakers both from Cyprus and from the international community.

In 1994 intercommunal talks between Glafkos Clerides and Rauf Denktaş—the elected presidents of southern and northern Cyprus, respectively—broke down after achieving no concrete results. Only in mid-1997 were the talks resumed. Of great concern to the international community is the escalating arms buildup by the Republic of Cyprus. Greek Cypriot military spending in 1997 had been $2 million per day. A five-year rearmament program introduced in 1997 will increase that amount. Meanwhile,the Republic of Cyprus finalized a deal to purchase highly sophisticated, Russian-made, long-range anti-aircraft missiles. Greek Cypriot leaders say that this degree of military readiness is necessary to meet the threat posed by tens of thousands of Turkish troops stationed in northern Cyprus. Increasing friction along the Attila Line adds to the world's concern that Cyprus is a potential hot spot.

> *"The response from Turkish Cypriot security forces was disproportionate to the threat posed by the protesters, notwithstanding the unauthorized entry of the protesters into the buffer zone."*
>
> Glyn Davies
> U.S. State Department spokesperson

ALONG THE ATTILA LINE

August 1996 brought the most widespread violence along the Attila Line since 1974. Early in the summer of 1996, the Cyprus Motorcycle Federation from the Republic of Cyprus announced plans to protest the lost right of free movement throughout the island. European, North American, and Greek Cypriot motorcyclists would bring worldwide attention to the boundary dividing Cyprus.

On August 2, 1996, motorcyclists left Berlin, Ger-

During a Greek Cypriot festival, tanks carrying sophisticated missiles rolled down a Nicosia street. International observers worry about the buildup of weapons in both the Republic of Cyprus and the TRNC.

© Patrick Robert/Sygma

many—chosen as a starting point because Berlin was formerly a divided city but was reunited in 1989. Hundreds of riders cruised across Europe and then boarded ships for Cyprus. Once in Cyprus, the group added 7,000 Greek Cypriot motorcyclists. On August 11, the riders planned to cross the Attila Line and travel to Kyrenia—a city on the northern coast of the TRNC.

The proposed motorcycle rally drew strong objections from Turkish Cypriot leaders. Immediately upon hearing of the motorcyclists' intention, the TRNC government warned that riders would be turned back at the Turkish Cypriot cease-fire line. If necessary, violence would be used to protect the border. The UN kept close watch on all developments as the date drew near. Finally, on August 10, the UN advised the Republic of Cyprus government to prevent the motorcyclists from attempting the last leg of the ride. The riders' plans to violate the cease-fire lines threatened to erupt into a major military situation.

On the morning of August 11, President Clerides called a meeting with the president of the Cyprus Motorcycle Federation and top police officers. They decided to call off the final, symbolic portion of the ride to preserve the 1974 cease-fire.

Although news of the rally's official cancellation was announced in Nicosia at a gathering of the motorcyclists, some riders were determined to press on with their goal. After leaving the stadium where they had been assembled, bands of motorcyclists headed toward various destinations along the buffer zone. At one spot, Republic of Cyprus police officers removed barriers at the Greek Cypriot cease-fire line, allowing some 350 cyclists to cross into the UN buffer zone. The riders advanced to the Turkish Cypriot cease-fire line. The demonstrators started fires as they went. They verbally insulted the Turkish troops and the Turkish Cypriot police along the Turkish Cypriot cease-fire line. UN peacekeepers were able to defuse the situation, and neither side incurred injuries. In their report of the event, the UN credited Turkish and Turkish Cypriot forces with restraint and criticized the Republic of Cyprus police for not controlling the Greek Cypriot demonstrators.

Reuters/Costa Kyriakides/Archive Photos

On August 11, 1996, demonstrators and police from the TRNC fatally injured Anastasios Isaak, a Greek Cypriot who, along with hundreds of others, had entered the UN-operated buffer zone near the eastern city of Dherinia. The Greek Cypriot–Turkish Cypriot clashes were the worst since partition in 1974.

But in other areas of the island, the demonstrations did not end peacefully. The worst violence occurred in Dherinia near the eastern coast. In the morning, Greek Cypriots peacefully demonstrated, asking to deliver a petition to the Turkish Cypriot checkpoint. The TRNC refused to accept the petition. Shortly before noon, about 1,000 persons—among them 300 motorcyclists—were escorted by the Republic of Cyprus police to the Greek Cypriot cease-fire line. The police spread out along the line but did not monitor the checkpoint. Demonstrators entered the UN buffer zone through the checkpoint and approached the Turkish Cypriot cease-fire line.

Meanwhile, Turkish forces let 1,000 persons—armed Turkish and Turkish Cypriot demonstrators and Turkish Cypriot police—disperse along the Turkish Cypriot cease-fire line. Then Turkish forces allowed them to enter the UN buffer zone. The sides soon clashed as Turkish troops, Turkish Cypriot police, and demonstrators responded with violence to

Greek Cypriot verbal insults and stone throwing.

From behind the Turkish Cypriot cease-fire line, Turkish Cypriot police fired upon Greek Cypriot demonstrators. With iron bars and bats, demonstrators from the TRNC set upon Greek Cypriots in the buffer zone. Anastasios Isaak, a 24-year-old Greek Cypriot, was beaten to death with clubs and rocks by a group of attackers that included three Turkish Cypriot police officers. Recorded on video, his brutal death was played back for international newscasts. In addition to the one Greek Cypriot death, 54 Greek Cypriots, 17 Turkish Cypriots, and 12 UNFICYP members were injured in Dherinia.

On August 14, following Isaak's funeral, more than 200 Greek Cypriot demonstrators returned to the Greek Cypriot cease-fire line. The Republic of Cyprus police were not effective in preventing their entry into the UN buffer zone. Demonstrators placed a wreath and a Republic of Cyprus flag on the spot where Isaak had died and then began throwing stones at the Turkish forces. UNFICYP was beginning to move Greek Cypriot demonstrators out of the buffer zone when a Greek Cypriot split off from the others and ran to the Turkish Cypriot checkpoint.

AP/Wide World Photos

Greek Cypriot demonstrators and UN soldiers dragged Isaak's body off the field, as intercommunal violence continued to rage throughout the zone.

Reuters/Costa Kyriakides/Archive Photos

On the day of Isaak's funeral, a Greek Cypriot named Solomos Solomou left the safety of the UN buffer zone and ran to the nearby Turkish Cypriot checkpoint. He shinnied up the flag pole with the intention of removing the Turkish flag. Blue-helmeted UN soldiers advised him to retreat. Turkish or Turkish Cypriot security forces shot at Solomou, who later died of his wounds.

He escaped capture and crossed the Turkish Cypriot cease-fire line. He climbed a flag pole with the intention of removing the Turkish flag. Turkish or Turkish Cypriot forces killed him and then fired into the crowd of demonstrators. Gunfire injured two Greek Cypriot citizens and two UNFICYP members. Five other civilians and two Republic of Cyprus police officers suffered other types of injuries.

SAYS WHO?

The UN blamed both sides for the violence in Dherinia but came down more heavily on the TRNC, saying the Turkish Cypriot police and Turkish forces used more force than called for by the situation. This was also the opinion of the U.S. State Department.

After the August events, strong accusations flew back and forth between Presidents Clerides and Denktaş. Each accused the other of twisting the facts in order to ensure that his respective government appeared to be in the right.

"The Greek Cypriot decision introduces a . . . destabilizing element . . . in the region. . . . This new missile system threatens to take the arms build-up on Cyprus to a new and disturbing . . . level."

Nicholas Burns
U.S. State Department spokesperson

According to Clerides, the demonstrations were the spontaneous action of unarmed Greek Cypriot citizens and foreign motorcyclists. He claims the Republic of Cyprus police and government attempted to prevent the demonstrations, but the motorcyclists could not be deterred. He accuses Denktaş of importing from Turkey some 2,500 members of a terrorist group called the Grey Wolves. Clerides states that politics motivated the importation of terrorists to attack peaceful demonstrators. The clash was engineered to create the appearance, which he claims is false, that Greek Cypriots and Turkish Cypriots can't live together.

The International Affairs Agency of the TRNC presents a very different version of events. The agency accused Clerides of cooperating with a plan drafted in Athens, Greece, by the Greek and southern Cypriot intelligence agencies. The motorcyclists were not acting independently, as Clerides stated. They had the backing of not only the Greek and Greek Cypriot governments but also of the Orthodox Christian Church. The church of the Greek Cypriots, which traditionally has had close ties with the nationalist movement, supported the riders' cause and helped raise funds for the rally.

The TRNC government accused the Greek and Greek Cypriot intelligence agencies of desiring a violent border incident to inflame world opinion against Turkey and the TRNC.

The TRNC government also claims that two days before the rally they received warning of the motorcyclists' preparations for an armed attack. The TRNC requested UN assistance to investigate. A search of the home of a high-ranking member of the Cyprus Motorcycle Federation uncovered a stash of dynamite, chains, iron bars, and Molotov cocktails. The reason the UN pressed the Republic of Cyprus to cancel the rally, TRNC officials claim, was to prevent the intended showdown.

Cypriots frequently hear several very different versions of the same event. Leaders of each government in Cyprus refer to the information released by the other community's media as

"Our flag is holy and sacred. We will never allow any hands on our flag. If they stretch their hands to our flag, they will be broken."

Tansu Ciller
former Foreign Minister of Turkey

propaganda. But in addition to government-issued news, Cypriots read reports of interactions with the other community in privately owned newspapers. Many of these sources, which operate in both the north and the south, also have politically motivated slants. It's often hard for those within and outside Cyprus to find out the truth.

POLITICAL STALEMATE

Many from each ethnic community are frustrated by the lack of progress toward a settlement. They believe that the situation in Cyprus, although difficult, should not be impossible to settle if politicians had ordinary citizens' interests at heart. Some Cypriots believe their leaders aren't listening because they are more interested in cooperating with the respective homeland or the international community.

Some Cypriots on each side of the Attila Line distrust their own leaders and the leaders of the other ethnic community. Elections in the Republic of Cyprus and in the TRNC reveal Cypriots' frustrations. Turnover of the Republic of Cyprus pres-

Cyprus: An International Issue

Many experts believe that if violence erupts in Cyprus, Turkey and Greece might go to war. The Cyprus problem and other tensions have brought the two countries to the brink of battle several times in recent years. Although Turkey and Greece are historical enemies, in the 1950s they became defensive allies when each country joined the North Atlantic Treaty Organization (NATO). More than a dozen other countries, including the United States, belong to NATO, an alliance to assure the mutual defense of member-countries.

Should Greece and Turkey go to war, fellow NATO members would be faced with a dilemma: What position should the organization take when countries within its ranks turn against one another? Furthermore, conflict within the organization weakens NATO's appearance of unity, raising questions about its strength and commitment to mutual defense.

Two other international organizations have much invested in a settlement in Cyprus. The United Nations (UN) has maintained thousands of troops on the island since 1964. Patience is waning as Cyprus appears no closer to a solution, and large numbers of the UN force have been withdrawn. In addition to the peacekeeping force, the UN secretary-general has conducted extensive negotiations between the leaders of the Greek Cypriot and Turkish Cypriot communities.

The European Union (EU) has become a major player in the conflict because the Republic of Cyprus has applied for full membership. This organization's decisions could change the political stability of the eastern Mediterranean. Some EU member-countries had objected to allowing the Republic of Cyprus to speak for the Turkish Cypriots. But in part due to pressure from Greece—an EU member—the organization has said it will consider Cyprus's membership regardless of the progress of negotiations. Turkish Cypriot leadership has strongly objected to the Republic of Cyprus joining the EU until a federal settlement is in place. In fact, the TRNC has threatened to unite with Turkey if the EU admits the Republic of Cyprus.

© Gino Russo

© Gino Russo

Top and above: *Both ethnic communities engage in propaganda, which influences how Cypriots view and behave toward those from the other community.*

idency has been frequent. In 1993 Clerides took over as president when he won the election by a narrow margin.

Denktaş has occupied the presidency in northern Cyprus since independence was declared in 1976. Some Turkish Cypriots resent the control he has over the politics of the TRNC. Many Turkish Cypriots feel that their voices are being diluted by the large number of Turks who have immigrated to Cyprus from the mainland since 1974. According to these Turkish Cypriots, they further feel that Denktaş permits primarily the Turks who will support him to immigrate.

Regardless of Cypriots' misgivings about their leaders, Cypriots' hopes are raised as Denktaş and each successive Greek Cypriot president approach the negotiating table. Although foreign relations do play a role in island politics, leaders of the Republic of Cyprus and the TRNC are also accountable to their respective Cypriot constituency. To retain their positions, politicians must not alienate voters by conceding too much to the other side.

Territorial Tensions

Cyprus's leaders are at odds over how to resolve territorial issues that arose with the island's division in 1974. Greek Cypriots protest the loss of three rights: to own property, to settle, and to move freely anywhere on the island. Some Turkish Cypriot officials insist that their community's safety depends on Cyprus staying bizonal (split into ethnic zones). They stand firm on their demand that one zone remain under Turkish Cypriot authority.

The Republic of Cyprus government and some elements of the Turkish Cypriot community claim that the TRNC government manufactures incidents to create anti-Greek Cypriot feeling among the Turkish Cypriot population. Turkish Cypriot leaders use this alarm to justify maintaining separate zones and to defend Turkey's continued military presence. The leaders of the Republic of Cyprus say the purpose of the TRNC's strategy is to provide a stepping-stone for the final goal of the Turkish Cypriot and Turkish governments: incorporating northern Cyprus under Turkey's flag.

According to the United Nations, freedom of movement within a country is a universal human right. Turkish Cypriot leaders allege, however, that they are justified in restricting this right to serve an even more sacred human right—to live without fear for their survival.

In each ethnic community, citizens have strong opinions about how major issues are resolved. For instance, a large portion of the voters living in southern Cyprus are refugees who formerly resided north of the Attila Line. Many of the displaced Greek Cypriots want to return to their northern villages and cities, where they still own property and have emotional ties. These Greek Cypriot voters sincerely want the negotiators to reach a settlement quickly. But they also insist that the Republic of Cyprus government remain firm in its demand that Cypriots be allowed to settle anywhere on the island. Many in the TRNC feel just as strongly that they cannot accept a settlement requiring Turkish Cypriots to live in mixed or adjacent settlements because their lives may be endangered. Adding to the anger of Greek Cypriots who want to return to the north is Denktaş's claim that this matter is not up for negotiation.

With the island's division in the 1970s, most children and many young adults in Cyprus have never met a Cypriot of the other ethnicity. From their leaders, the news media, and their older relatives they hear contradictory information. Turkish Cypriot children are told by government leaders that Greek Cypriots and Turkish Cypriots cannot live together. Some of their ethnic kin, however, tell them that not all Greek Cypriots participated in the violence against Turkish Cypriot enclaves. They recall the days before the conflict when members of the two ethnic communities interacted peacefully.

Greek Cypriot leaders emphasize to the world that Greek Cypriots and Turkish Cypriots can live together peacefully again. But this can happen only if Turkish Cypriot leaders send home Turkish troops and allow

Greek Cypriots to return to the property from which they were uprooted. Despite the government's assurances of the possibility of peaceful coexistence, Greek Cypriot newspapers often describe Turkish Cypriots in negative terms. Some even run banner headlines that read "The Best Turk is a Dead Turk."

Examining the shared history of Greek Cypriots and Turkish Cypriots—from its beginnings to the present day—will help explain the strong emotions of each community. Such an examination may also reveal the long-standing difficulties of finding a solution. ⊕

An abandoned house lies within the UN buffer zone in Nicosia. Decades of meetings have yet to yield a settlement acceptable to Greek Cypriots and Turkish Cypriots or to their homelands—Greece and Turkey.

CHAPTER

2

THE CONFLICT'S ROOTS

Cyprus has been inhabited since about 6000 B.C. The first residents sailed to the island from the Middle East or from Asia Minor (the peninsula on which most of present-day Turkey is located). The settlers built small villages along the coast and later moved inland to clear farmland on the heavily forested Mesaoria Plain.

Copper—*kypros* in the Greek language—may have given Cyprus its name. About 2000 B.C., islanders discovered underground deposits of copper ore in the foothills of the Troodos Mountains. They melted down the ore and combined it with tin to create bronze, a durable metal that went into weapons and tools. The island's cities grew wealthy from trade in bronze goods, pottery, grain, wine, and jewelry. Cyprus also benefited from its location on busy trade routes between Asia Minor, the Middle East, and Africa.

Beginning about 1500 B.C., the wealth and strategic location of Cyprus brought several waves of invasion and foreign colonization. In search of fertile land, Greeks first voyaged to Cyprus around 1200 B.C. from their homes in the Aegean basin.

© Trip Photographic Library/C. Galley

From the remains of Vouni, an ancient Persian palace in northern Cyprus, the rugged landscape stretches to the sea.

Over time, they established 10 separate city-states on the island.

The Greeks were followed by Phoenicians, Assyrians, Egyptians, and Persians. By the fifth century B.C., Greek Cypriots were engaged in a doomed revolt against harsh Persian rule. Under these successive rulers, Cypriots were obligated to pay heavy tributes to foreign treasuries.

The Persians easily put down the revolt. They rewarded their allies, the Phoenicians, and put them in charge of the island's largest cities.

Corbis-Bettmann

By the fourth century B.C., *the Persians had awarded Cyprus to their allies the Phoenicians. With Greek aid, the Greek Cypriot king Evagoras overthrew Phoenician-Persian rule on the island and helped sack Tyre* (above), *the Phoenician commercial hub in what would become Lebanon.*

About this time, King Evagoras of Salamis, a Greek Cypriot city-state, instituted the use of the Greek alphabet and encouraged Greek studies. Under his leadership, he united the Greek Cypriot city-states. Evagoras sought help from Athens, a powerful city-state in Greece, and the Greek and Greek Cypriot forces overthrew Persian rule. Although Persia regained control of Cyprus after several years, Evagoras had drawn Cyprus into a closer political and cultural alliance with Greece.

In 333 B.C., Alexander the Great, the king of Macedonia—then a region that included parts of northern Greece—campaigned against the Persians. The Cypriots helped Alexander conquer Tyre, an important Phoenician port in what is now southern Lebanon. Alexander's victories led to Cyprus's liberation from Persia. Alexander ruled Cyprus until his death in 323 B.C., when control of the island passed to Ptolemy, one of Alexander's generals. The Ptolemaic dynasty (the series of rulers descended from Ptolemy) governed Cyprus for the next 250 years. During this time, many people from Greece made pilgrimages to Paphos, a city on Cyprus's western shore that had become a center of Greek culture and religion.

ROME AND CHRISTIANITY

During the time of the Ptolemaic dynasty, the Republic of Rome in Italy was extending its control to the eastern Mediterranean.

Romans overthrew the Ptolemaic dynasty and in 58 B.C. incorporated Cyprus into the province of Cilicia, which also included land in southeastern Asia Minor.

In A.D. 45, an apostle named Paul arrived in Cyprus and preached a new one-god faith called Christianity, which had originated in the Middle East. Accompanied by Barnabas, a Cypriot citizen, Paul converted the island's Roman governor. Cyprus became the first Roman province to be ruled by a Christian, and the new religion gradually replaced the ancient Greek cults.

In the fourth century, the Roman emperor Constantine made Christianity the official religion of the empire. Constantine set up headquarters for the Greek-speaking portion of the Roman Empire in the city of Byzantium, renaming it Constantinople (modern-day Istanbul, Turkey). Rome continued to function as the capital of the Latin-speaking (western) half of the empire.

In time each half of the empire had its own church. The western, or Roman Catholic, branch had its seat in Rome, where the Catholic pope resided. The eastern, or Orthodox, division had several independent churches headed by partriarchs, or archbishops, who ruled from

Archive Photos

Born in Tarsus (a city in modern Turkey), Paul initially opposed Christianity but later devoted himself to converting people to the faith.

SCALA/Art Resource

Cyprus thrived during the prosperous reign of the emperor Justinian (in brown cloak, holding bowl), *who ruled the Byzantine Empire in the sixth century A.D.*

Cultural and Tourism Office of the Turkish Embassy

By painting with white ink on gold, a Turkish artist produced this ornate verse from the Koran, the holy book of the Islamic religion.

several religious centers. Both Greece and Cyprus followed the practices of the Eastern Orthodox Church.

Meanwhile, successive invaders were gradually weakening the empire, and the Western Roman Empire fell in the mid-fifth century. Cyprus remained a possession of the Eastern Roman (or Byzantine) Empire, under which it continued to flourish.

As early as 431, Orthodox religious leaders in Cyprus requested that the island be allowed to establish its own independent church. Because Cyprus had played an important role in early Christianity, permission was granted in 488 for an autonomous Church of Cyprus. This meant that the seat of authority for the Greek Cypriot religion would be in Cyprus and that Orthodox Cypriots would have their own archbishop who would lead Greek Cypriots' spiritual life. The Byzantine emperor who approved the church's establishment also allowed the Orthodox leaders in Cyprus to run much of the civil government. Having control in both the spiritual and secular spheres, the church became the largest landowner and the single most powerful institution on the island.

RISE OF ISLAM

In the seventh century, the prophet Muhammad founded the Islamic religion in the Middle East. Muhammad inspired his followers, called Muslims, to spread the new faith through military conquest. Cyprus came under a massive Arab attack in the mid-seventh century. Over the next 300 years, Arab raiders massacred many thousands of Cypriots and destroyed all of Cyprus's Byzantine churches. But by 965 Byzantine forces had prevailed over the Arabs in Asia Minor, and Cyprus was brought back into the Byzantine Empire. In the meantime, conflict between the Roman Catholic and the Orthodox Church led to a permanent division of the Christian faith's two major branches.

During the eleventh century, the Seljuk Turks—a Muslim people—had conquered much of the eastern Mediterranean from Islamic Arab clans. The Seljuks took control of Palestine, a Middle Eastern region also called the Holy Land. (Modern Palestine is smaller than it was during Seljuk rule, when the region covered present-day Israel, the West Bank, southern Syria, and a larger portion of Jordan.) Jerusalem—a city of strong religious importance for the Judaic, Christian, and Islamic faiths—fell under Seljuk rule. The Seljuk Turks, using even more extreme measures than the Arab Muslims did, tried to prevent Christians from traveling to this religious site.

This Orthodox church was built in the tenth century. By this time, Cyprus had returned to Orthodox control following centuries of Islamic rule.

To restore Jerusalem to Christian control, Europe's popes and kings mounted a series of military campaigns from the 1000s to the 1200s. Cyprus's location in the eastern Mediterranean made the island an important staging ground for these campaigns, which became known as the Crusades.

Although Roman Catholic and Orthodox troops joined forces against the Muslims, the Crusades didn't end the rivalry between the eastern and western branches of Christianity. In 1191, during the Third Crusade, ships belonging to the Roman Catholic English king Richard I (the Lion-Hearted) were wrecked off the coast of Cyprus. Orthodox Byzantine troops raided the ships. In retaliation, Richard conquered the island.

Richard left his own representative in charge of the island but soon lost interest in holding it when the Cypriots revolted. To help finance his Crusade, the English king sold Cyprus to a religious military order known as the

Wayland Picture Library

The English king Richard I conquered Cyprus in the late twelfth century but held it for only a short time. He was followed by a series of European overlords whose combined rule lasted almost 400 years.

Knights Templars. Troubled by popular uprisings against their harsh rule, the Templars soon turned Cyprus over to Guy de Lusignan, a French noble, in May 1192.

Lusignan, a Roman Catholic, established a new dynasty that would rule Cyprus for the next 300 years. The Lusignans banished the Church of Cyprus's archbishop and replaced him with Catholic bishops. Although the Roman Catholic Church outlawed Orthodox practices and forced the Cypriots to adopt the Latin (western) Mass, Cypriots practiced the Orthodox rite in secret and clung to their traditional Greek culture.

The Crusades ended in failure in 1291, when Muslim forces captured Acre, the last Crusader outpost in the eastern Mediterranean. Many Crusaders fled to Cyprus, where they were granted estates by the Lusignans.

A new threat in the region—the rise of the Ottoman Turks of Asia Minor—taxed Lusignans' defenses. Cyprus came to depend on Venice and Genoa, wealthy Italian states with large trading fleets and military forces in the Mediterranean. Cyprus officially became a Venetian possession in 1489. For the Cypriots, Venetian rule proved no better than that of the Lusignan kings. The island's longtime residents were the economic underclass, while prosperous Cypriot ports were under the control of Venetian merchants.

Meanwhile, Ottoman armies were sweeping from Asia Minor into southeastern Europe. The Ottoman Turks, like the Seljuk Turks, were Muslims. They conquered Constantinople and overthrew the Byzantine Empire. Turkish sultans (rulers) made the city, which they renamed Istanbul, their capital. Turkish rule spread quickly to Greece as well as to the eastern Mediterranean. During the late fifteenth century, the Turks began staging destructive raids in Cyprus.

In 1570 the Ottoman Empire landed a large force near Limassol. The Venetians had only a small army to protect their cities. In Nicosia some 20,000 people died, and the city fell within two months. After a long and bloody siege, the Turks captured Famagusta in August 1571. That year Cyprus became an Ottoman province.

© Gino Russo

After the Ottoman Turks established themselves on the island in the sixteenth century, Orthodox churches and Islamic mosques (houses of prayer)—such as these examples in Limassol—existed side by side in Cypriot cities.

TURKISH CYPRIOT ROOTS

The Turkish conquest drove Venetian merchants and fleets from Cyprus. Although many Cypriots were killed during the Ottoman conquest, living conditions in Cyprus improved under Turkish rule. The Turks established the millet system of rule, which they used throughout the Ottoman Empire. Under this idea of governing, instead of suppressing or trying to convert the religious communities in the lands they had acquired, the Ottomans allowed a conquered people to practice their faith. The Turks bestowed upon the community's religious leaders the duties of civil administration. As long as they complied with the sultan's taxation code, Greek Cypriot Orthodox priests administered Cyprus's cities with considerable freedom.

The millet system reestablished much of the power the Church of Cyprus had enjoyed during Byzantine days. Greek Cypriots, who had continued to cling to their faith during Lusignan and Venetian rule, were now allowed to follow the teachings of their religion. In 1575 the Orthodox archbishop of Cyprus returned to serve as the ethnarch (religious and political leader) of the Greek Cypriots.

The Turkish conquest brought to Cyprus a wave of immigrants. Turkey's policy was to maximize the productivity of its newly acquired lands, and Cyprus was too sparsely populated to be an asset. So the Ottomans encouraged the Turkish soldiers who had helped conquer Cyprus to settle on the island. About 20,000 soldiers stayed. However, still more people were required to increase Cyprus's economic output, and Turkey transferred thousands more of its population to work in Cyprus's fields and mines.

Over time, Greek Cypriots and Turkish Cypriots formed two distinct communities, divided by different languages (Greek and Turkish), religions (Orthodox Christian and Islam), and customs. Nevertheless, the two groups lived in ethnically mixed or adjacent villages and managed to share the island in relative peace.

GREEK REBELLION

By the early 1800s, the Ottoman sultans were unable to rule the vast realm effectively from Istanbul, and the expense of defending their far-flung territories gradually emptied the Ottoman treasury. Greek Cypriots and Turkish Cypriots alike began protesting heavy Ottoman taxation. At the same time, seeing the growing weakness of the Ottomans, Russia and Britain began vying for control of sea routes in the eastern Mediterranean.

In the 1820s, an anti-Ottoman revolt—which came to be known as the Greek War of Independence—erupted in Greece and in Greek-speaking provinces throughout the Ottoman Empire. Although Cyprus had never been ruled by Greece, many Greeks and Greek Cypriots considered the island to be Greek territory, tied to Greece by age-old bonds of language, culture, and religion. Suspecting a plot among the religious leaders of the Greek Cypriots, the Turkish governor ordered the arrest and execution of the ethnarch, Archibishop Kyprianos, and of several other Greek Cypriot leaders. By the 1830s, the Greeks had succeeded in recapturing part of their former lands from the Ottomans. Cyprus, however, remained under Ottoman control.

Over time, Greek Cypriots and Turkish Cypriots formed two distinct communities, divided by different languages . . . , religions . . . , and customs.

The Greek revolt inspired a growing sense of nationalism among Greek Cypriots. Most members of the Greek Cypriot community favored enosis, unification with Greece. Orthodox leaders believed that enosis offered Cyprus the best chance of throwing off Ottoman rule.

BRITISH ADMINISTRATION

While Greek Cypriots were rallying behind enosis, Russia was attempting to gain power in the Mediterranean. Russia's efforts greatly alarmed the Ottoman Empire as well as Britain, which conducted much of its overseas trade through the Suez Canal in Egypt. This situation prompted Turkish and British leaders to strike a deal over Cyprus in 1878.

In exchange for full administrative control over the island, Britain agreed to protect the Ottoman Empire against Russia. Cyprus remained an Ottoman possession, but the agreement allowed the British to use Cyprus as a strategic military base that would protect Britain's possessions in the Mediterranean.

Pro-enosis Greek Cypriots opposed British rule but for the most part did not react violently. Some Orthodox leaders felt that Britain would soon hand Cyprus over to Greece because the British had supported the Greek independence movement of the 1820s.

The British administration in Cyprus established the Legislative Council, which was made up of three Turkish Cypriots, nine Greek Cypriots, and six representatives appointed by the British high commissioner. Most votes taken by the council resulted in a deadlock. Because of the Greek Cypriot push for enosis, Turkish Cypriot representatives—who greatly feared being ruled by their homeland's longtime rival—allied with the six British appointees. In effect, the British high commissioner, who had the power to cast the deciding vote in case of a tie, controlled the council.

The British opened new hospitals, built roads, and made some investments in the island's economy. They encouraged the island's communities to maintain ties to their ethnic heritages. Perpetuating the distance between the communities—a strategy called "divide and rule"—proved advantageous to the British for quite some time. The islanders' separate cultural loyalties meant that Greek Cypriots and Turkish Cypriots would not unite to rise up against colonial rule.

Under British rule, separate Greek Cypriot and Turkish Cypriot educational systems were established. They ensured that the island's population would maintain strong cultural connections to either Greece or to Turkey. Schools taught students in Greek or in Turkish, with English as a second language. Textbooks and teachers—imported from Greece or from Turkey—passed on cultural biases.

The drive for enosis was intensifying among Greek Cypriots, who believed that British rule would eventually lead to independence from Turkey and to union with Greece. In a 1903 vote, the Greek Cypriots in the Legislative Council called for enosis. But the vote was strongly opposed by the

The Illustrated London News

In 1878 Greek Orthodox priests blessed the British flag as it was raised in Nicosia, an event that signified the beginning of British rule on the island. Speaking for the Greek Cypriot community, one of the bishops greeted the British high commissioner by saying, "We accept the change of Government inasmuch as we trust that Great Britain will help Cyprus . . . to be united with Mother Greece, with which it is naturally connected."

An Unexpected Outcome

While in power, the British governed according to the "divide and rule" method, under which each group was encouraged to retain its cultural identity, that is to stay divided. In so doing, the British thought Cypriots would be unlikely to join together to rise up against them. Divide and rule, however, resulted in each ethnic community and its homeland developing stronger ties to one another. During the 1800s, when a strong nationalist movement occurred in many countries, these bonds made Cyprus a likely spot for nationalism to take hold.

Greek nationalists wanted to reunite all lands that had formerly been ruled by Greeks—a movement called enosis (Greek for union). And although Cyprus had never been governed by Greece, people of Greek heritage had long lived on the island. The goal of enosis was to bring together all territory inhabited by ethnic Greeks under a centralized Greek government. Both Greek Cypriots and Greeks worked toward union.

Turkish Cypriot council members. The British members also objected, fulfilling their obligations to Turkey as well as safeguarding Britain's own interests in Cyprus's strategic geographical location.

WORLD WAR I AND AFTER

In the summer of 1914, World War I broke out in Europe between the Central Powers, led by Germany, and the Allies, which included Great Britain. The Ottoman Empire allied with Germany at the start of the war, prompting the British to annex (take over) Cyprus in November. In the next year, Britain offered Cyprus to Greece to entice Greece to enter the war on the Allied side. The Greek government declined, however, and chose to stay neutral until 1917, when it joined the Allies. But by that time Britain had withdrawn its offer.

The Allies defeated the Central Powers in the fall of 1918. The Ottoman Empire collapsed, and a new government headed by Kemal Atatürk established the Republic of Turkey in 1923. That same year, Great Britain and Turkey signed the Treaty of Lausanne, which formally granted Cyprus to Britain.

The British were officially in charge of Cyprus, so Greek Cypriots believed that the British would allow a vote on self-rule. But for Britain, Cyprus still occupied a strategic position. As in the late 1800s, Britain teamed up with the Turks to oppose Mediterranean expansion of the Soviet Union (the **Communist**-run state that had replaced the Russian Empire). The Turkish government strongly opposed Cyprus's independence, which they believed would soon lead to enosis. In addition to concern for Turkish Cypriots, who would be subjected to direct Greek rule, Turkey did not want Greece to rule the territory nearest its southern shore.

The British government decided to ignore the wishes of Greek Cypriots and to keep control of the island. Britain made Cyprus a crown colony in 1925, replacing the high commissioner with an appointed governor. Despite this change in status, which put Cyprus under direct British rule, Greek Cypriots

The Illustrated London News

continued to desire enosis. Distrust and resentment rose among Greek Cypriots, who believed that the British administration and the Legislative Council favored the interests of Turkish Cypriots. In addition, a worldwide economic depression that began in 1929 hurt trade and caused rising unemployment and a drop in the Cypriot standard of living.

When the British governor attempted to raise taxes by decree in 1931, Greek Cypriots staged a violent riot in Nicosia, during which the British Government House was burned down. The rebellion spread and triggered revolts in one-third of Cyprus's villages. The British responded by suspending the Cypriot constitution, abolishing the Legislative Council, and banning Greek Cypriot and Turkish Cypriot political parties. British decrees censored the press, gave the police the authority to search persons and their homes, and deported 10 Greek Cypriot leaders who

The Illustrated London News

Top: *Enosis, the desire for unification with Greece, became a rallying cry for Greek Cypriots in Cyprus. But Britain refused to give up control of the island.* Above: *Riots that erupted in Nicosia in 1931 resulted in the destruction of Government House, the headquarters of the British governor.*

were involved in the disturbances. The governor assumed dictatorial power. To break the ties islanders felt for their homelands and to prevent conflict between Cyprus's ethnic communities, the British suppressed the teaching of Greek and Turkish history. They also banned people from flying Greek or Turkish flags in public. Later the British would put into effect a law requiring the governor's approval of an archbishop elected by the Orthodox community.

The restrictions put on Cypriots crushed most unrest in Cyprus, but they did not stop the Greek Cypriot drive for enosis. Throughout the 1930s, Greek Cypriot exiles in foreign capitals campaigned for a vote on **self-determination** (the right to choose political status) for Cyprus. Most British leaders—who believed that Cypriots were better off under British rule than they would be under Greek control—underestimated the value Greek Cypriots put on enosis. At the same time, Britain was preoccupied by events on the European continent, where Nazi Germany,

Turkish Cypriot Resentments

The British government's restrictions on Cypriots' freedoms applied to both ethnic communities, even though Turkish Cypriots had not participated in the 1931 rioting. This punishment angered the Turkish Cypriot community, which already resented British rule. Although the combined Turkish Cypriot and British votes in the Legislative Council defeated the Greek Cypriot vote, the alliance was out of mutual necessity rather than harmonious relations.

In the early 1920s, after the fall of the Ottoman Empire and before the Turkish Republic had been established, the British had taken away from Turkish Cypriots rights to run their own schools and courts. Adding to the tension was the increase of poverty on Cyprus, a complaint that the two ethnic communities shared. Isolation and fear because of their smaller numbers within the Cypriot population caused many Turkish Cypriots to want closer ties with the Republic of Turkey. This desire persisted even though the Turkish leader Kemal Atatürk had made it clear that he was not interested in acquiring Cyprus. "Although our nationalism loves all Turks . . . with a deep feeling of brotherhood, and although it desires with all its soul their wholesome development, yet it recognizes that its political activity must end at the borders of the Turkish Republic."

Cultural and Tourism Office of the Turkish Embassy

Kemal Atatürk (left, with hand on railing), *first president of the Republic of Turkey, steered clear of acquiring Cyprus, despite the wishes of Turkish Cypriots.*

under Adolf Hitler, was preparing for war.

WORLD WAR II AND ITS CONSEQUENCES

World War II broke out in 1939, when Germany invaded Poland, prompting Britain to declare war on Germany. In 1940 Italy invaded Greece. The Greeks succeeded in pushing out the Italians but were then set upon by the Germans.

During the war, thousands of Cypriots volunteered to join the British forces, and Cyprus became an important naval and air force base for British troops fighting in the Middle East and North Africa. Many Greek Cypriots hoped that the alliance of Britain and Greece would lead to Cypriot independence after the war, which ended with Germany's defeat in 1945.

After World War II, the nations of Western Europe feared that the Soviet Union, which had put Communist parties in control of Eastern Europe, would take control of Europe and the Mediterranean. A military alliance with the United States, the only nation that matched the Soviet Union in military

Imperial War Museum

During World War II (1939–1945), Cyprus proved strategically important for military campaigns in North Africa and the Middle East. Above: *Workers unloaded supplies from a British army truck at Famagusta.* Below: *These Cypriot volunteers and their mules formed part of the British army's Pack Transport Company, Cyprus Regiment.*

Imperial War Museum

Archbishop Makarios III (right), *an influential leader of the enosis movement, was born Mikhail Khristodoulou Mouskos in western Cyprus in 1913. The son of a poor shepherd, Mouskos entered a monastery at the age of 12 and was ordained in 1946 as an Orthodox priest. After studying in Greece and the United States, Mouskos returned to Cyprus in 1948 and became the bishop of Kitium. In 1950 he succeeded Makarios II as archbishop of Cyprus. Taking the name Makarios III, he traveled widely pleading the case for enosis.*

Archive Photos/Express Newspapers

might, seemed the best protection Western Europe had against a Soviet invasion.

As a result, in 1949 the United States, Britain, and their allies formed the North Atlantic Treaty Organization (NATO). Under this agreement, member-nations agreed that an attack against one country in NATO would be considered an attack against all members. In 1952 Greece and Turkey—longtime enemies—joined NATO, therefore becoming allies.

In the meantime, Britain relaxed the emergency measures initiated in Cyprus in the 1930s and, among other things, allowed exiled Greek Cypriot leaders to return. The Orthodox community elected a strongly pro-enosis bishop, Makarios II, to become archbishop.

In January 1950, Orthodox leaders arranged to have a plebiscite (popular vote) to demonstrate support for enosis among Cypriots. The Greek Cypriot response was 96 percent in favor of union with Greece. Although many Greek Cypriots strongly believed in uniting with Greece, the Orthodox Church influenced Greek Cypriots to vote in favor of enosis. Churches posted pro-enosis signatures and punished with excommunication those who did not support the cause. In June Makarios II died. His successor, Makarios III, carried on the enosis campaign with increasing popular support.

CHAPTER 3

ENTRENCHED POSITIONS

In July 1951, Makarios III met with a Greek colonel named Georgios Grivas, a native of Cyprus and a hero of the Greek resistance forces during World War II. Grivas strongly backed the enosis cause. Grivas favored a **guerrilla** campaign against the British. He began the preliminary steps of forming an underground movement that he and Makarios would eventually name the National Organization of Cypriot Fighters (abbreviated from the Greek language as EOKA). Grivas recruited many EOKA members from two youth organizations that Makarios had formed. At this point, however, Makarios was still using diplomacy and negotiation to achieve enosis.

Makarios directed his efforts toward persuading Greece to present to the UN the Greek Cypriot majority's desire for self-determination. He eventually succeeded, and in August 1954 Greece requested that the organization discuss Cyprus's political status. Numerous countries in Asia and Africa had won independence from colonial rule in the years following World War II. Many UN members believed that Cypriots also had the right to choose their own political future.

UPI/Corbis-Bettmann

In the 1950s, Georgios Grivas organized the anti-British guerrilla group known as the EOKA.

Britain insisted that self-determination for Cyprus was an internal British problem and should not concern other countries. Turkey also strongly objected to a UN review. Turkish leaders worried about the status of Turkish Cypriots should Cyprus be allowed self-determination.

If the British were to withdraw, Turkish Cypriots wanted the island to be partitioned into two ethnic zones, each of which would unite with its homeland. They thought this policy of *taksim*, or "double enosis," would be a fair solution, allowing self-determination for each of Cyprus's ethnic communities.

Even before the UN handed down a decision, Makarios had become convinced that stronger measures would be necessary to remove the British, and Grivas had set up headquarters in Cyprus. In the fall of 1954, as Cypriots awaited the UN's answer, Britain was tightening its hold on the island. The British had lost important military bases in Egypt that protected its interests in the Suez Canal Zone and needed Cyprus's strategic location in the Middle East more than ever.

AP/Wide World Photos

In the Kyrenia Mountains, British soldiers searched villagers suspected of belonging to the EOKA, which had become somewhat legendary for its ability to cause damage and destruction throughout the island, while avoiding capture by British paratroopers.

The UN decision "not to consider the problem further for the time being, because it does not appear appropriate to adopt a resolution on the question of Cyprus" inflamed pro-enosis Greek Cypriots. Greece also reacted angrily. Greek premier Alexandros Papagos complained that Greece's allies had betrayed the country. In response Greece closed its airports to its NATO allies Britain and Turkey.

ANTI-BRITISH MOVEMENT

When the UN decision was handed down, Greek Cypriot anger exploded. According to Henry Hopkinson, minister of state for the colonies, "There are certain territories in the Commonwealth which, owing to their peculiar circumstances, can never expect to be fully independent." Greek Cypriot confidence that enosis could come through political negotiation collapsed, and frustration levels escalated.

The British threatened advocates of enosis with up to five years' imprisonment, but the warning did nothing to squelch the anti-British feelings. Greek Cypriots responded with strikes, demonstrations, and rioting. In Limassol British police officers killed two people while firing upon Cypriot crowds for the first time to control severe rioting.

On April 1, 1955, Grivas launched the EOKA campaign, assaulting Nicosia, Famagusta, Larnaca, and Limassol. The group targeted British radio stations, military bases, and government offices. The EOKA guerrillas, armed with weapons that had been smuggled in from Greece, hid in the Troodos Mountains. Partisans traveled to cities or villages to conduct assassinations or bombings and then retreated to the mountain caves and other hiding spots where they were able to avoid capture by police. Besides direct attacks against the British, the EOKA also incited many Greek Cypriots to demonstrate.

In August Britain took an unusual step. Until this point, Britain had not discussed the problems in Cyprus with other governments. But after months of attacks, Britain invited officials from Greece and Turkey to London to discuss the island's future. The homeland of each Cypriot ethnic community stood firm: Turkey wanted to forbid enosis; Greece expected enosis to be allowed. The Tripartite Conference, as this meeting was known, broke up without resolution. In fact, instead of finding ways to decrease the tensions in Cyprus, the Tripartite Conference succeeded only in increasing hostilities between Greece and Turkey.

In Nicosia, as Sir John Harding took up his post as governor of Cyprus, Greek Cypriots armed with stones and bottles struggled against the police who tear-gassed the crowds. Makarios, using the tactic of passive resistance, called for the resignation of Greek Cypriot officials to hamper government operations. Many village mayors responded by withdrawing from office, cutting off government links throughout the island.

[Said Henry Hopkinson], "There are certain territories in the [British] Commonwealth which . . . can never expect to be fully independent."

In November 1955, a state of emergency was called, and reinforcements for Britain's troops arrived. By December 12,000 British troops were stationed in Cyprus. In addition, hundreds of British police officers had been brought in to replace the EOKA sympathizers within the Cypriot police force. In many incidents, children or teenagers instigated attacks against the British.

It was clear that a portion of the Greek Cypriot population was determined to accomplish enosis in any way possible. It was equally clear that the Turkish Cypriot community was going to resist and would increase its resistance as the push for enosis continued. If union was achieved, Turkish Cypriots feared that the Greek government would seize their property and expel their community from the island as Greeks had done in other lands they had conquered from Turks.

As anxieties grew among Turkish Cypriots, their feelings of identification with Turkey intensified. "Cyprus is Turkish" became a popular slogan in the Turkish Cypriot community, and many felt that Turkey should regain rule of the island if the British withdrew. At this point, however, Turkey did not offer to aid its Cypriot kin. A number of Turkish Cypriots realized that the success of British security

Archive Photos

British soldiers arrested a teenage schoolboy for his involvement in the anti-British movement in Cyprus.

forces was all that stood between them and enosis. They joined the British ranks as auxiliaries.

On most occasions, EOKA members directed their violence at the British. But many Greek Cypriots were Communists, advocating the Soviet Union's system of government. Their political beliefs put them at odds with those in the enosis movement, because Greece was strongly anti-Communist. The EOKA asked Greek Cypriot Communists to stand aside as the guerrillas fought for union with the homeland. Extremist pro-enosis supporters often killed Turkish Cypriots or Greek Cypriots who stood in the way of union with Greece.

PROPOSALS FIZZLE

As tensions in Cyprus were mounting, Governor Harding and Archbishop Makarios were trying to negotiate Cyprus's future. In March 1956, after five months of talks, the two had reached a deadlock, and they discontinued the meetings. Britain had agreed that self-determination would happen but refused to commit itself to a time frame. Britain's maneuverings around the issue frustrated Makarios.

Within days after the meetings broke up, the British charged Makarios of abetting the anti-British violence and exiled him and several other Orthodox church leaders. This action backfired. The situation in Cyprus became even more violent as the no-holds-barred EOKA leader Grivas stepped in to fill the vacuum left by Makarios's exile.

Meanwhile, Cyprus's importance as a British military base fell after Britain lost the Suez Canal Zone. The British intensified their attempts to find a solution agreeable to both Cypriot communities so they could pull out of the island, but little headway was made.

British colonial leaders submitted a proposal in December 1956 called the Radcliffe Report. This plan included the option of self-determination in the future but also contained measures that would safeguard the Turkish Cypriot community. Turkey and Turkish Cypriots approved the plan. Greece rejected it. Greek Cypriots complained that, being the majority, they should not have to give in to Turkish Cypriot demands for protection.

Britain then suggested that the island be partitioned between Greece and Turkey. Turkish Cypriots quickly supported this concept, adopting a new slogan: "partition or death." This proposal also pleased Turkey. Turkish Cypriots would probably fare better under this arrangement than under enosis, Turkey believed, and a Turkish zone in Cyprus would create a buffer between a Greek zone on the island and mainland Turkey.

In April 1957, Makarios was allowed to go to Athens, Greece, where he was received with a hero's welcome by thousands of pro-enosis Greeks. He also voyaged to New York, where he brought the cause of Cypriot self-determination before the UN once again.

Meanwhile, in Cyprus violence escalated as Greece increased its military assistance to the EOKA. Pro-enosis Greek Cypriots also put their energies into removing signs of Turkish culture on the island in preparation for union with Greece. The Greek Cypriot majorities on municipal councils, which the British had set up to run local government services, wanted to make the island more Greek. The councils voted to change the names of those streets and squares that were Turkish to Greek. Only Greek flags were allowed to fly over town halls. Turkish Cypriot sections of cities were neglected. By mid-1957, disheartened Turkish Cypriot city councilors resigned, ending jointly run municipalities.

Turkey had been balancing its desire to help support Turkish Cypriots with the request by Britain that other countries refrain from military action in Cyprus. Turkey decided to enter the playing field. It justified its intervention by pointing out that Greek military support and Makarios's attempts to involve the UN had turned Cyprus into an international issue. In November 1957, a Turkish colonel founded the Turkish Resistance Organization (abbreviated from the Turkish language as TMT). Turkey sent military advisers and weapons to the underground organization to counter the increasing threat posed by the EOKA. The TMT coalesced existing Turkish Cypriot underground groups into a central organization that could coordinate activities and create ties with sympathizers in Turkey. The TMT also strove to inspire confidence among Turkish Cypriots.

With well-equipped underground forces in each Cypriot community, violence soared in 1958. Tensions between Greece and Turkey increased.

STEPS TO INDEPENDENCE

The crisis in Cyprus worried the nations of western Europe and the United States. The bitter rivalry between Greece and Turkey weakened the NATO alliance in a region where NATO and the Soviet Union were in intense competition. Turkey had threatened war against Greece if Greece forced enosis upon Turkish Cypriots. British leaders concluded that a negotiated settlement of the Cyprus problem was necessary to holding together NATO and to keeping a balance of power in the Mediterranean.

In June 1958, another British proposal—the Macmillan Plan—was rejected by Greeks and Greek Cypriots, who likened it to partition because it suggested adopting separate legislative bodies for a seven-year period during which a more permanent solution could be found.

Although the Macmillan Plan was not accepted by Greek Cypriots, most of them realized that Britain and Turkey would not allow enosis. In December Greece and Turkey began negotiations over Cyprus in which independence rather than enosis or partition was considered. In February 1959, Greek premier Constantinos Karamanlis and Turkish premier Adnan Menderes met in Zurich, Switzerland, to hammer out a plan for an independent Cyprus.

Talks moved to London, where Archbishop Makarios; Fazil Küçük, the Turkish Cypriot leader; and British prime minister Harold Macmillan joined the discussions. Makarios voiced some objections to the plans, but he signed the Zurich-London Agreements, which consisted of three treaties. Under the Treaty of Establishment, Britain would keep control of two military bases in Cyprus. Under the Treaty of Alliance, Greece and Turkey could each station troops on the island—950 and 650, respectively. Also included in the Treaty of Alliance was the go-ahead for the new government to recruit a Cypriot army. Under the Treaty of Guarantee, Britain, Greece, and Turkey agreed to uphold the constitution and the island's territorial integrity. This meant enosis as well as partition of Cyprus would be prohibited.

The treaties would form the basis of the new Cypriot constitution. During the lengthy process of drafting the constitution, Makarios returned to Cyprus for the first time since his exile in 1956. Underground leader Grivas, who rejected anything short of enosis and

AP/Wide World Photos

The British exiled Makarios in 1956, but he returned to a lavish welcome in Nicosia three years later.

therefore broke with the archbishop, returned to Greece in December 1959.

The Cypriot constitution made provisions for a Greek Cypriot president and a Turkish Cypriot vice president. Both heads of state had the power to veto legislation passed by the House of Representatives, which would be made up of 35 Greek Cypriot and 15 Turkish Cypriot legislators. Elections for all offices would be done in separate communal balloting, with each community voting for only the government leaders who represented its ethnic kin. Appointments to a council of 10 ministers would be split between the communities seven to three, with Greek Cypriots having the majority of ministers. Separate Greek Cypriot and Turkish Cypriot communal chambers would administer matters of religion, culture, and education. And a force of 2,000 Cypriots—60 percent Greek Cypriot and 40 percent Turkish Cypriot—would make up the military.

EARLY INDEPENDENCE

The negotiators of the constitution had tried to strike a political balance between the two Cypriot communities. They also attempted to provide Britain, Greece, and Turkey—NATO allies—with a face-saving chance to resolve the Cyprus problem. The result, however, was that the ethnic makeup of the island became the basis of the new political and legal systems in Cyprus.

On August 16, 1960, Cyprus officially became an independent state. In the summer and fall, the people of Cyprus celebrated. For the first time in more than 2,000 years, their island was free of control by foreign rulers.

As British colonial officials left the island and the new government took office in Nicosia, many Cypriots were hopeful of a peaceful future. But reluctance from some factions to accept the political balance called for in the constitution and differing interpretations of the document planted the seeds of a new and more violent conflict.

Even though enosis was constitutionally outlawed, many Greek Cypriots still desired it. Enosis also remained a popular cause among the people of Greece and a goal that many Greek politicians supported. Among those Greek Cypriots who shared the dream of eventual union with Greece were the first elected president, Archbishop Makarios, and many high-ranking members of the Cypriot government. They viewed Cyprus as Greek territory and believed the newly independent government was only temporary. Although most Greek Cypriot members of Cyprus's government united behind Makarios, not all within the general Greek Cypriot population supported the president. Some Greek Cypriots who had been involved in the EOKA resented Makarios because he had sold short of reaching enosis. On the other

[Until independence] Identification with Turkey intensified. "Cyprus is Turkish" became a popular slogan in the Turkish Cypriot community.

end of the spectrum were Greek Cypriot Communists who were against enosis.

Turkish Cypriots abandoned their demand for the island's partition and readily accepted independence, hoping that the built-in safeguards of the new constitution would protect them. Fazil Küçük, elected by the Turkish Cypriot voters, took office as the republic's vice president.

Aware of the continued pro-enosis talk among their Greek Cypriot counterparts, some Turkish Cypriot leaders worried that the constitution might not be upheld. Should the constitution fail, some Turkish Cypriots feared that Greek Cypriots would expel them from their land. And even if they were not forced to leave their property, other Turkish Cypriots believed that the government would help Greek businesses and farmers to compete unfairly.

As Makarios appointed Greek Cypriot ministers, Turkish Cypriot suspicions increased. They were especially wary of the president's appointment of Polykarpos Yorgadjis to the position of minister of the interior—the official responsible for internal security on Cyprus. Yorgadjis had been deeply involved with the EOKA and had participated in the intercommunal violence that had preceded independence. A Turkish Cypriot leader reported that Yorgadjis's attitude toward Turkish Cypriots was clearly revealed in a speech the interior minister gave while in his native village in which he said, "There is no place in Cyprus for anyone who is not Greek, who does not think Greek and who does not constantly feel Greek."

There is no place in Cyprus [Yorgadjis said] for anyone who is not Greek, who does not think Greek and who does not constantly feel Greek.

CLASHES AND PROPOSALS

Distrust between Greek Cypriot and Turkish Cypriot government leaders soon brought disagreement. One strongly debated issue was the makeup of the new Cypriot army. President Makarios and Greek Cypriot officials wanted to set up a totally integrated force, with Greek Cypriots and Turkish Cypriots serving together on every level. Vice president Küçük and Turkish Cypriot officials agreed to integrated troops at the higher levels but wanted separate Greek Cypriot and Turkish Cypriot units in the army's lower ranks.

The vice president claimed that Greek Cypriot leaders planned to fill all 150 officer slots available to their community with ex-EOKA members. Küçük feared that ex-EOKA army officers would follow orders to attack Turkish Cypriot enclaves scattered around the island. Küçük wanted separate units of Turkish Cypriot soldiers to provide protection should the army turn against the Turkish Cypriot population. Küçük also foresaw practical difficulties in uniting troops that spoke different languages and practiced different faiths. According to the Turkish Cypriot interpretation of the constitution, separate ethnic troop units were allowed under the law.

In October 1961, Makarios asked the Council of Ministers to vote on a measure to integrate all levels of army units. Greek Cypriots, who held the majority of cabinet posts, passed the motion. Küçük used his executive veto to stop plans for the integrated army. As a result, Cyprus did not develop an army of its own. Makarios blamed Küçük for the government's inability to fulfill the Treaty of Alliance's mandate that Cyprus form an army. The Greek and Turkish units stationed on the island in accordance with the treaty became the dominant armed forces in Cyprus.

In 1962 the government found itself nearly paralyzed. It disagreed over the collection of taxes, over the proportion of Turkish Cypriots and Greek Cypriots hired as civil servants, and over the existence of separate local governments. On the last matter, the Cypriot Supreme Constitutional Court ruled in favor of the Turkish Cypriots in April 1963. The court decided that the constitution required separate municipalities in Cyprus's five largest cities. Makarios, who believed that allowing separate city governments was the same as partition, ignored the court's ruling.

Misgivings between Greek Cypriots and Turkish Cypriots increased as both sides struggled over legislation. During arguments over measures that came up for consideration, each side accused the other of trying to violate the requirements of the Treaty of Guarantee. Greek Cypriots said Turkish Cypriots were trying to partition the island. Turkish Cypriots saw each piece of legislation proposed by Greek Cypriots as an attempt to move the island closer to enosis.

Meanwhile, forces on Cyprus prepared for a fight. As early as 1961, Greek Cypriots had begun building up a secret army under orders from President Makarios and under the supervision of Interior Minister Yorgadjis. In addition to arms and explosives that were smuggled from Greece, weapons from the EOKA campaign of the 1950s were still circulating among enosis supporters in Cyprus. Training for the Greek Cypriot secret army took place in the Troodos Mountains, and about 10,000 troops had been readied by December 1963. In addition to the secret army, gangs who had retained their loyalty to Grivas were ready to commit violent acts against the Turkish Cypriot community. Preparing to seal off Turkish Cypriot enclaves in case of Greek Cypriot attacks, the TMT trained members and smuggled in weapons and advisers from Turkey. The stage was set for war.

In 1963 Interior Minister Yorgadjis was in charge of drawing up a top-secret outline called the Akritas Plan. Putting the plan into action would bring control of the island into Greek Cypriot hands and would prepare Cyprus for enosis. One of the first goals of Greek Cypriot leaders and Greek army officers involved in the plan was to convince the world that Cypriot citizens hadn't approved the Zurich-London Agreements.

To garner support, Greek Cypriot officials said that the agreements would have been rejected had they been presented to the Cypriots for a vote. They also claimed that Makarios, as the Greek Cypriots' representative, had been pressured by Britain,

Turkish Republic of Northern Cyprus

Members of the Turkish Resistance Organization (TMT), posed in 1963, during the early phases of intercommunal violence.

Turkey, and Greece into signing the agreements.

Another objective for plan proponents was to convince the world that Greek Cypriots, who made up four-fifths of the Cypriot population, were not satisfied with the 1960 constitution, although Makarios had participated in drafting it. Pro-enosis Greek Cypriot leaders wanted to persuade other nations that the constitution was flawed and would always lead to political deadlock. To accomplish this, they needed to demonstrate that constitutionally permitted actions taken by the Turkish Cypriot vice president, legislators, and ministers were preventing the government from functioning. As an example, they pointed to Vice President Küçük's use of the veto. On the one occasion when he'd used this power, he had derailed plans to establish a totally integrated army, which had been approved by Greek Cypriot ministers.

Greek Cypriot officials claimed that the vice president's veto power allowed the minority to prevent the majority's wishes. In addition, requiring separate majorities of Turkish Cypriot and Greek Cypriot politicians to pass legislation in areas such as defense and taxes enabled the minority community to force its wishes upon the majority.

To move forward, Greek Cypriot officials said, the constitution must be amended to give the majority the political dominance it needed to run an effective government. Greek Cypriot officials also needed to reassure the international community that proposed changes to the constitution would not endanger the reasonable rights of Turkish Cypriots.

The Akritas Plan outlined how Greek Cypriots should react if a Turkish Cypriot uprising took place. Cypriot security forces would "suppress this forcefully in the shortest possible time" to prevent foreign intervention. After resistance was crushed, Greek Cypriot officials would push through the amendments. They would also cancel the Treaty of Guarantee (which obligated

Archive Photos/Express Newspapers

Turkish Cypriots elected Fazil Küçük as the first vice president for independent Cyprus. He was wary of efforts by Greek Cypriots to combine administration of the island's ethnic communities, fearing that superior Greek Cypriot numbers would eventually lead to Greek Cypriot domination.

Turkey, Britain, and Greece to prevent either enosis or taksim). Without the Treaty of Guarantee, outside intervention to prevent enosis would be outlawed, and Greek Cypriot officials could put enosis up to the public for a vote. The Greek Cypriot majority, which was influenced by the pro-enosis Orthodox Church, would pass it.

On November 30, 1963, Makarios presented 13 amendments to Vice President Küçük. Turkish Cypriot members of government were told to respond by the end of December. The first proposed change—and perhaps the most objectionable to Turkish Cypriots—would remove the veto power of the president and the vice president. Other amendments would unify the justice system and city governments; would remove limits on the number of security forces; and would change the ratio of Greek Cypriots to Turkish Cypriots in the civil service, security forces, and the army to reflect the proportions within the population. Legislation that had required separate Greek Cypriot and Turkish Cypriot majorities would pass on the basis of a simple majority.

The reactions of Cypriots to the proposed amendments reflected an important distinction in the way each ethnic group perceived its relationship to the other. To Greek Cypriots, Turkish Cypriots were a minority within the total Cypriot population. Greek Cypriots felt that a group's power should be proportional to its percentage of the population.

But Turkish Cypriots did not view the Cypriot population as one pool of people. They resented the term minority when it was used to describe their community. Instead, they understood the founding of the Republic of Cyprus as having been between two equal partners. Although Turkish Cypriot numbers within the population were smaller, they did not agree that the voice of the more populous Greek Cypriots should dominate.

As expected, Turkish Cypriot government members strongly opposed the proposals. But even before they had formally responded, Turkey—which as a guarantor power had the obligation to maintain the constitutional status quo—rejected the measures on December 16. As the month wore on, tensions mounted between the two ethnic communities, and security measures on the island were increased.

TEMPERS EXPLODE

On December 21, 1963, Greek Cypriot police officers stopped a Turkish

Cypriot woman in the Turkish Cypriot quarter of Nicosia and asked for her identification papers. According to Turkish Cypriot reports, the officers also attempted a body search. A group of angry Turkish Cypriots swarmed, and the police fired their weapons, killing two people. Violence escalated as other members of the Greek Cypriot security forces, the EOKA, the TMT, and Greek Cypriot and Turkish Cypriot citizens became involved. The next night, heavy firing occurred in the Turkish Cypriot quarter of Nicosia and in Omorphita, a suburb of the capital with a substantial Turkish Cypriot population. Greek Cypriot extremists and security forces isolated Turkish Cypriots in Nicosia from the outside world and cut their lines of communication. Early reports, generated by Greek Cypriot communication channels, stated that Turkish Cypriots were attempting to overthrow the government and were embarking on a massive slaughter of the Greek Cypriot community. These broadcasts inflamed Greek Cypriots, who fought with increasing fervor. Akritas Plan supporters disarmed and detained Turkish Cypriot police officers while Greek Cypriot members of security forces were armed and mobilized.

Intercommunal violence quickly spread throughout the island. Within a few days, foreign reporters began arriving. Journalists found Turkish Cypriot citizens clustered in large public buildings under the protection of the TMT, who struggled to fight Greek Cypriot security forces and EOKA attackers. Greek Cypriot security had often cut off supplies of food and medicine. In some cases, Greek Cypriots had burned Turkish Cypriot villages or riddled homes with bullets. Greek Cypriot forces killed Turkish Cypriot citizens of all ages. Fighting was especially heavy in Nicosia and along the road between the capital and Kyrenia.

OUTSIDE INTERVENTION

On December 24, Turkey appealed to Britain and Greece to join together militarily to restore peace in

Panoramic Images

Turkish Cypriot villagers fled from the violence that erupted in late 1963.

Cyprus. The same day, they sent word to Makarios, offering to establish a joint peacekeeping force. On December 25, when Makarios had not yet responded, Turkey flew jets low over Nicosia. Turkey also moved its troops—stationed in Cyprus in accordance with the Treaty of Alliance—to the road between Kyrenia and Nicosia. According to Turkey, this move was made to protect an area heavily populated by Turkish Cypriots. The Republic of Cyprus government viewed it as a way of ensuring a clear land route from Kyrenia, on the Cyprus coast nearest Turkey, to Nicosia. The following day, Makarios agreed to allow the guarantors—Greece, Turkey, and Britain—to establish a force in Cyprus. He also requested that the UN look into the acts of aggression conducted by Turkey.

Responsibility for the peacekeeping force fell on Britain, the most neutral of Cyprus's three guarantors. Allied to both Turkey and Greece through NATO, Britain didn't want its actions in Cyprus to offend either homeland. The thinly spread force, consisting of about 3,000 British troops, could not prevent all outbreaks of violence, most of which were initiated by Greek Cypriot forces against the Turkish Cypriot enclaves.

To contain violence in Nicosia, the British established the Green Line (so-called because it was drawn on a map with a green pen), which split the city into ethnic zones. The British decision to divide the capital angered Makarios. He claimed that Britain was an accomplice in the Turkish Cypriot goal to partition the island. He resented that British troops would not help the Cypriot government disarm the TMT, which continued to protect Turkish Cypriot enclaves. Despite foreign ob-

Archive Photos

A Turkish Cypriot high in the hills points his machine gun at a road leading to Kyrenia.

Archive Photos/A.F.P.

As part of the United Nations Forces in Cyprus (UNFICYP), Canadian troops arrived in Limassol in 1964.

servers' accounts to the contrary, Makarios persisted in claiming that Turkish Cypriots were instigating the island's disturbances. Makarios was infuriated that the peacekeeping force protected Turkish Cypriots as they fled from areas of mixed population to Turkish Cypriot strongholds.

In mid-January 1964, representatives from both Cypriot ethnic communities met with negotiators from Greece, Turkey, and Britain at the London Conference. The heated discussions ended with Greek Cypriots sticking to their demand that the constitution be amended and with Turkish Cypriots insisting that the island be partitioned. NATO's stability was threatened as agitation increased between Turkey and Greece. Britain could no longer support the peacekeeping force in Cyprus and asked that a new force be developed. The UN agreed to send troops and began organizing the United Nations Forces in Cyprus (UNFICYP).

Violence continued to flare. In mid-February, attacks against the Turkish Cypriot quarter of Limassol, a large, mostly Greek Cypriot city on Cyprus's southern coast, were particularly severe. Not long afterward, Turkey issued an ultimatum to Makarios stating that all attacks on Turkish Cypriots must end or Turkey would take unilateral action in Cyprus. Turkey believed the Treaty of Guarantee gave it the right and obligation to act alone if necessary to maintain the 1960 constitution. Turkey prepared its troops, but the United States sent a navy fleet to block them from moving into Cyprus. Turkey pulled back, and the first UN forces soon began arriving.

UNFICYP troops took up positions between Greek Cypriot and Turkish Cypriot forces in several cities. But with fighting on the island scattered in many locations, the UN troops could do little to stop it. Other factors added difficulty to the UN's peace mission. For example, the Cypriot government—run solely by Greek Cypriots at this point—had not given the UN force full freedom of movement on the island. The UN needed to consult with government officials before they could set foot in restricted areas. Another hurdle was the restriction of using force solely in self-defense. This limited the peacekeepers' impact on many clashes between the ethnic communities.

UPI/Corbis-Bettmann

Intercommunal fighting caused civilian deaths on both sides. These Turkish Cypriots were killed during a skirmish near Nicosia.

GREECE BACKS KIN

Enosis remained Makarios's goal. In April 1964, the president met with Greek premier Georgios Papandreou, who agreed to back the enosis movement with arms and troops. Makarios began to set up a National Guard. Turkish Cypriot officials claimed that this organization was illegal. Nevertheless, President Makarios appointed a lieutenant-general from the Greek army to head the force and filled its ranks with Greek Cypriot draftees. Papandreou fulfilled his promise, and weapons and almost 10,000 Greek troops arrived secretly to bolster the National Guard's ranks.

Meanwhile, Turkey again threatened to attack Cyprus because of ongoing violence against Turkish Cypriots. U.S. president Lyndon B. Johnson was concerned about the likelihood of war between NATO allies if Turkey were to invade. The United States had provided weapons to Turkey, but not for use against Cyprus. Johnson warned Turkey that

Archive Photos

Left: *In the hills of Cyprus, Turkish Cypriots mounted an around-the-clock watch to warn of any Greek Cypriot troop movements.* Below: *With President Makarios in the background, Georgios Grivas spoke to crowds after his return to Cyprus in June 1964.*

Archive Photos/Express Newspapers

Turkey would violate its agreement with Washington, D.C., if it used U.S. arms in an aggressive act. Once again, Turkey stopped short of entering Cyprus.

In mid-June, Papandreou sent Grivas—who had not been back to Cyprus since his split with Makarios in 1959—to command the Greek army stationed in Cyprus. Grivas soon took over the National Guard as well. Although responsible to Greece rather than to Makarios, Grivas made many of his decisions independent of either authority. With Grivas at the helm and many Greek officers leading its troops, the National Guard became an arm of the Greek military in Cyprus.

At the same time, the United States increased its efforts to prevent Greece and Turkey from escalating tensions in Cyprus. Under UN mediation, the Greek

United Nations

Greek Cypriots took up positions near the Castle of St. Hilarion, a tenth-century fortified monastery that was a stronghold of the Turkish Cypriots during the 1963–1964 violence.

and Turkish premiers met with Dean Acheson, President Johnson's envoy, in Geneva, Switzerland. The United States set forth a solution called the Acheson Plan at the Geneva Conference. This plan would allow enosis but would require Greece to make some concessions to Turkey and to the Turkish Cypriots. Greece and the Greek Cypriots rejected the plan.

By August 1964, Grivas had made plans for the National Guard to conduct extensive military operations in northwestern Cyprus, especially near Cape Kokkina. The TMT was also preparing for a fight, smuggling arms and troops from Turkey into northern Cyprus. On August 6, the National Guard overtook UN observation posts, forcing the peacekeepers to retreat. Guard members attacked Turkish Cypriot villages by land and from the water. The heavy attacks continued through the next day.

On the night of August 7, Turkish jet fighters buzzed the National Guard forces and fired warning rockets into the sea. Turkey prepared troops for attack and also positioned troops along its border with Greece. Because Turkey had not followed through on past threats, President Makarios didn't expect Turkey to act this time. When the National Guard's battle against Turkish Cypriot villages continued on August 8, Turkey made good on its threats.

Using rockets, and bombs, Turkish jets fired on National Guard troops. The Greek government was concerned that Turkey had upped the stakes and ordered the National Guard to stop all attacks, but the forces continued fighting. Again on August 9, Turkey bombed National Guard positions and Greek Cypriot villages where reinforcements were gathering. In these villages, Greek Cypriot civilians as well as National Guard troops were killed or injured. Finally Makarios and Grivas accepted the immediate cease-fire demanded by the UN Security Council.

Examining Allegations

Reports vary greatly about the motives behind the violence that occurred between Cypriot communities in 1963 and 1964. Each ethnic community blames the other for engineering the first stage of Cypriot segregation. According to Turkish Cypriots, the Greek Cypriot leadership wanted Turkish Cypriots to reject the proposed amendments so Greek Cypriots could implement the Akritas Plan, the goal of which was to force out Turkish Cypriots from government and then to unite with Greece.

Greek Cypriots claim that Turkish Cypriot leaders were trying to partition the island, which they say has long been on Turkey's agenda. According to the Greek Cypriots, Turkish Cypriot leaders withdrew from government to accomplish taksim, or partition. Greek Cypriot sources also declare that Turkish Cypriot extremists committed some of the violence against their own people and blamed Greek Cypriots to create fear of Greek Cypriots among Turkish Cypriots. This fear, manufactured by the pro-partition Turkish Cypriot leadership, forced Turkish Cypriots to leave their villages and to relocate in areas heavily populated by their ethnic kin.

Turkish Cypriot refugees gathered in camps near Nicosia to escape the fighting.

Corbis-Bettmann

CHAPTER 4

THE PRESENT CONFLICT

Between December 1963 and August 1964, 364 Turkish Cypriots and 174 Greek Cypriots were killed. Several hundred missing Turkish Cypriots were never accounted for. During these months, 25,000 Turkish Cypriots became refugees when they left their homes to join ethnic kin in densely populated Turkish Cypriot areas. In more than 100 villages, the entire Turkish Cypriot population fled, leaving personal property behind. Reports reveal that organized Cypriot extremists from both communities, as well as ordinary citizens, acting out of fear and anger, participated in the violence. Greece and Turkey also played a large role, supporting their respective ethnic kin with arms and troops.

Although atrocities were committed by both ethnic communities, observers have placed more blame on Greek Cypriots. In a push to achieve enosis, they ignored the human cost of their goal. Not all Greek Cypriots supported the cause, however, and many did not participate in the violence. Speeches made by President Makarios during this period clearly reveal that he continued to support enosis. Reports vary regarding the extent he planned, condoned, or perpetuated violence as a means to fulfill the dream.

TURKISH CYPRIOT ENCLAVES

Tension between the ethnic communities remained high. Turkish Cypriots continued to crowd into enclaves, which the TMT protected. Turkish Cypriots put up barriers to keep out Greek Cypriot security forces, which in turn put up roadblocks around the enclaves to keep in Turkish Cypriots. The Greek Cypriot-run government censored mail sent to Turkish Cypriot enclaves. An economic embargo restricted materials—such as cement, sand, timber, and spare auto parts—from reaching Turkish Cypriot communities. The shortages not only hampered construction of new housing but also prevented an industrial economy from forming. Turkey ended up providing much of the money necessary to sustain its ethnic kin.

Facing page: *For thousands of years, Cyprus's proximity to three continents—Europe, Asia, and Africa—has made the island strategically important.*

MACEDONIA
TURKEY
BLACK SEA
Istanbul
GREECE
AEGEAN
SEA
ATHENS
TURKEY
ANKARA
NICOSIA / LEFKOŞA
CYPRUS
MEDITERRANEAN SEA
LEBANON
SYRIA
West Bank
ISRAEL
JORDAN
Gaza
Suez Canal
LIBYA
EGYPT
North Africa

ATHENS Capitals
Istanbul Major cities
International boundaries
Disputed international boundaries

GREEK CYPRIOT POLITICS

Meanwhile, another type of showdown was occurring in Cyprus. During the late 1960s, Makarios was experiencing his own difficulties. His dual roles as the Cypriot president and the Greek Cypriot religious leader were beginning to pull him in different directions.

According to Orthodox traditionalists, Makarios had a sacred duty to promote enosis through violence if necessary. Although Makarios still favored enosis, for the meantime he was willing to settle for independence and had rejected aggression as a means of achieving union with Greece. Makarios could see that an increasing number of Greek Cypriots were moving away from the strict teachings of the church. Many of this growing segment belonged to the Communist Party—the largest political party in Cyprus. To win elections and to retain his presidency, Makarios had to appeal to these voters, too. But the Communists were strongly opposed to enosis, and the pro-enosis traditionalists were extremely anti-Communist. The House of Representatives was still controlled by enosis supporters, however, and in 1967 it passed a resolution pledging the government's continued efforts to unite with Greece.

After 1964, Turkish Cypriots remained outside the Republic of Cyprus's government, which Greek Cypriots continued to operate in their absence. Greek Cypriots viewed as illegal the organizations Turkish Cypriots had set up to administer the Turkish Cypriot community. Turkish Cypriots viewed as illegal all legislation passed by a House of Representatives with only Greek Cypriot members.

Embassy of the Republic of Cyprus

Grivas defied Makarios's orders to stop attacks on Turkish Cypriot enclaves. He accused Makarios of treason for abandoning the enosis cause. Grivas's accusation drew many former EOKA extremists away from the president. In addition to attacking Turkish Cypriots, Grivas's supporters besieged fellow Greek Cypriots, mainly members of the AKEL, Cyprus's Communist Party.

Makarios asked Greece to reduce Grivas's powers, but Greece ignored Makarios's request. Meanwhile, on April 21, 1967, another blow surprised Makarios: the Greek military junta (committee) took over the elected government in Athens in a **coup d'état**. The former government had allowed Makarios a large degree of independence to accomplish enosis.

The military junta was strongly anti-Communist and disliked Makarios's tolerance of the Cypriot Communist

Party. In addition, they did not agree with the president's rigid approach to enosis. Makarios had been unwilling to give up any part of the island to Turkish Cypriots to bring about enosis. Instead, Makarios would delay enosis until it could be obtained on his own terms. The new Greek leadership perceived Makarios as inflexible and impractical. Determined to achieve enosis, the junta understood that compromises must be made. Knowing Makarios's reluctance to give in to Turkish requests, the Greek leadership began direct negotiations with Turkey for two main reasons. Firstly, patching up matters with Turkey would increase support for the junta, both within Greece and internationally. Secondly, maintaining thousands of Greek troops in Cyprus was expensive. Although the Greek leaders felt they had the spirit necessary to reach an agreement with Turkey, talks between the two NATO powers did not yield a solution.

AP/Wide World Photos

In 1967 a Greek Cypriot student carried a poster demanding the return of Grivas. Before being recalled to Greece, Grivas had used his control of the National Guard to attack Turkish Cypriots and to push for enosis.

TROUBLE FOR NATO

The junta had mixed feelings about Grivas. The folk hero's sporadic attacks against Turkish Cypriots had put Greece into an uncomfortable position during negotiations with Turkey. But the junta needed Grivas to control Makarios.

On November 15, 1967, under Grivas's direction, the National Guard launched a particularly heavy attack on Turkish Cypriots in two villages near Larnaca in southeastern Cyprus. While the battle progressed, the troops disarmed and cut the communications of UN forces in the area. Turkey once again prepared for a confrontation, this time against both Greece and Cyprus. Turkey issued an ultimatum to Greece with numerous demands, including that Grivas leave Cyprus. The Greek junta, knowing they did not have a choice, recalled Grivas from the island. Other demands were not met, and Turkey continued to prepare for war.

With war between two NATO members on the horizon, U.S. president Lyndon Johnson sent Cyrus Vance to join the negotiations. Vance helped defuse the situation, and Greece and Turkey reached a compromise. They agreed to reduce troops in

Cyprus to the numbers permitted by the Treaty of Alliance. As Greece withdrew its excess troops, Turkey was to break down its war preparations. Two other aims—that the Republic of Cyprus dissolve the National Guard and that the powers of UNFICYP be increased—never came about.

War had been avoided, but tensions in Cyprus continued. In December 1967, Turkish Cypriots, who saw themselves as a stateless people, set up the Provisional Turkish Cypriot Administration. Küçük headed its Executive Committee. The Legislative Assembly was made up of the 15 Turkish Cypriot members of the former dual House of Representatives and 15 members of the Turkish Cypriot Communal Chamber. The Supreme Court and lower courts would tend to the community's judicial needs.

They did not seek to be recognized as an official government, which would have violated the Treaty of Guarantee and the constitution. They claimed this administration would operate only "until such time as the provisions of the Constitution of 1960 have been fully implemented." But Greek Cypriot leaders interpreted this move as the first step toward partition, and the UN also disapproved of the Turkish Cypriot decision.

MAKARIOS'S UPS AND DOWNS

In early 1968, an election in the Republic of Cyprus returned Archbishop Makarios as president. He won with 96 percent of the vote, much of it from the AKEL. The DEK, a newly formed party that appealed to pro-enosis extremists, received only 2 percent of the vote. This result indicated that the majority of Greek Cypriots did not want enosis—or viewed the timing for it as wrong. In response, the small, radical pro-enosis element of Cyprus, in conjunction with the Greek junta, turned more to terrorism to accomplish its aim. As terrorism escalated, Makarios began leaning more toward the Communists for support, alienating anti-Communist members of government.

Makarios lifted the economic embargo against Turkish Cypriots in 1968 and began intercommunal talks. Makarios saw a benefit to broadening his power base by reconciling the ethnic communities in Cyprus. Glafkos Clerides, Makarios's representative, and Rauf Denktaş, the Turkish Cypriot representative, began weekly discussions.

Many Greek Cypriots, however, were content to live separately and to govern the island without input from Turkish Cypriots. The president's decision to expand his power base further splintered the Greek Cypriot community.

Many questioned Makarios's ability to maintain control of the government. Their fears were heightened by a

[Turkish Cypriots] claimed this administration would operate only "until such time as the provisions of the Constitution of 1960 have been fully implemented." But Greek Cypriot leaders interpreted this move as the first step toward partition.

failed assassination attempt in 1970 and by the return of General Grivas in 1971.

Backed by the Greek junta, Grivas founded his second underground Greek Cypriot group to promote the enosis cause. Grivas called his new group EOKA B. Unlike the original EOKA—whose purpose had been to free Cyprus from British rule—the EOKA B was established to oust Makarios.

Many EOKA B members came from the ranks of the original EOKA or from the Cypriot National Guard. Greece paid the salaries of those who joined the EOKA B and supplied the organization with arms and uniforms. A further threat to Makarios's rule came from the Cypriot police force, whose ranks over the years had become filled with pro-enosis extremists.

In the early 1970s, as Makarios's ability to maintain power came into question, he began to deal harshly with those who opposed his administration. In 1972 he established the Tactical Reserve Force (TRF) to protect the presidential palace in Nicosia as well as telecommunication lines, radio and television stations, and the international airport. This new police force was staffed with Greek Cypriots loyal to Makarios, who also came to depend on a **paramilitary** group under the control of socialist leader Dr. Vassos Lyssarides. Around this time, the president issued publications that advocated the overthrow of the Greek junta, whose threat Makarios began facing head on.

Of Makarios the Greek junta said, "[He should] step down and make room for those who . . . possess the realistic spirit needed for a final solution that will be both profitable to the nation and generally acceptable."

In the fall of 1973, the leader of the Greek junta—Colonel George Papadopoulos—was forced from power by his radical rival General Dimitrios Ioannides. Ioannides despised Makarios because of his willingness since 1968 to negotiate for a solution with Turkish Cypriot officials. A settlement between the ethnic communities, Ioannides felt, would postpone or prevent enosis entirely. Ioannides planned a coup against Makarios and cooperated with Grivas, who continued to carry out terrorist attacks. But in January 1974, Grivas died suddenly of a heart attack.

Makarios viewed Grivas's death as an opportunity to regain control of the island. He banned the EOKA B and ordered the surrender of all illegally held weapons.

On July 2, 1974, Makarios sent a letter to the Greek president, accusing the Greek government of plotting to take over Cyprus. Makarios also charged the junta with attempts against his life and demanded that the hundreds of Greek officers serving in the National Guard leave the island.

In response, the junta ordered the National Guard to overthrow Makarios. The coup—code named Operation President—began during the morning hours of July 15. National Guard tanks and troops surrounded the presidential palace in Nicosia. Nearly 200 members of the TRF defended the palace against heavy gunfire until more forces loyal to Makarios arrived. Shortly after the fighting began, Makarios slipped out of the back of the palace and went by car to Paphos, a city on the southwestern coast.

By early afternoon, Makarios's forces in Nicosia had almost been defeated. The National Guard had set the presidential palace on fire and had declared over the radio that Makarios was dead. After hearing these announcements several times, the commander of the TRF called a cease-fire.

In the midafternoon, the National Guard had sworn in Nikos Sampson—a passionately anti-Turkish Greek Cypriot—as Cyprus's new president. A puppet of the Greek military junta, Sampson had been a major player in attacks against the Turkish Cypriot enclaves during 1963–1964. With Sampson in charge, Turkish Cypriots' concern about their survival soared. Most Greek Cypriots also opposed this change in leadership but were powerless to challenge the alliance of Greek Cypriot extremists and the Greek junta.

But Makarios was not dead. After urging his followers to continue the fight, Makarios flew to London, where he felt he could do more for the Cypriots than he could on the island. Some fighting continued but it soon became clear that the National Guard had the upper hand. Lyssarides's pro-Makarios paramilitary group retreated to the Troodos Mountains and dispersed. Sampson's regime conducted house-to-house searches and disarmed, questioned, and arrested hundreds of Makarios supporters.

Simonpietri/Sygma

For a short time, Nikos Sampson acted as Cyprus's president after Makarios's overthrow in 1974.

During and after the coup, members of the National Guard and the EOKA B killed Greek Cypriots loyal to Makarios. The estimated number of Greek Cypriot casualties varies from a few hundred to more than a thousand. Many of the dead were not identified and were buried in mass graves.

TURKEY'S ACTIONS

On July 16, Turkey appealed to Britain for military help in restoring Cyprus's elected government. Britain was reluctant to step in for several reasons. It feared for the safety of its military personnel and had economic interests on the island. In addition, Makarios had asked Britain not to use force.

The United States was equally wary of becoming involved and did not condemn Greece's participation in overthrowing the island's elected government. Besides the dubious proposition of choosing to back one or the other NATO ally, siding with Turkey could put at risk U.S. military installations in Greece.

AP/Wide World Photos

U.S. Diplomacy: Summer 1974

After the Greek junta overthrew Makarios, the United States shuttled State Department representative Joseph Sisco between Athens and Ankara to prevent the outbreak of war between NATO allies. However, neither Turkey nor Greece knew exactly where the United States stood, partly because the United States hadn't taken strong measures to prevent the coup.

Some journalists attributed this lack of forcefulness in confronting the junta to U.S. interest in maintaining bases in Greece. Many anti-junta Greeks felt that, in looking after the U.S. military's concerns, the United States was sacrificing the wishes of the Greek majority. Other reports speculated that the United States had allowed the coup because Henry Kissinger, then head of the state department, didn't respect Makarios and was concerned that he was establishing relations with Communist countries.

No one was certain what the next move of the United States would be. The Greek junta felt the superpower should prevent Turkey from fulfilling its threats of military intervention. Greece insisted that the United States tell Turkey to stay clear of Cyprus. If the United States didn't cooperate, the Greek junta threatened to withdraw from NATO and to take away the U.S. bases. Turkey feared that the United States would give in to Greek threats and would recognize the new government of Cyprus. And U.S. recognition would go a long way toward legitimizing the Sampson regime in international opinion.

Turkey attempted to persuade the United States to oppose the regime and to support Turkey's proposed intervention. Turkish premier Bülent Ecevit assured the United States that Turkey "should be able to compensate for any weakness that ensues as a result of the Greek [NATO] withdrawal." Before the United States had a chance to act, Turkey, in what it called a peace operation, sent troops to Cyprus to remove the Sampson regime and to protect its ethnic kin.

The United Nations was also unwilling to condemn Greece. In fact, the only country that offered Turkey military aid was the Communist Soviet Union. By helping Turkey, the Soviet Union would achieve two goals. Firstly, the Soviet Union could help bring Makarios, who was sympathetic to the Communist cause, back to power in Cyprus. Secondly, the Soviet Union could drive a wedge in NATO—the defense organization set up to oppose Soviet power. Turkey did not take up the Soviet offer, but the prospect of an alliance between a NATO member and the Soviet Union caused serious concern among other NATO member-countries.

Instead Turkey put its armed forces on alert. It demanded that Greece withdraw its officers from Cyprus and remove Sampson from the presidency. Turkey further demanded that Greece guarantee the independence of Cyprus.

The Greek junta refused to negotiate. As July 20 dawned, an estimated 6,000 Turkish troops invaded Cyprus. Navy landing craft unloaded Turkish infantry and tanks on the island's northern coast. Paratroopers jumped from transport planes. Low-flying Turkish jets bombed Greek Cypriot military targets.

As the day wore on, Turkey gained control of Kyrenia and the road leading out of the port city to northern Nicosia, the capital's Turkish Cypriot quarter. Turkish gunfire and bombs hit many of the intended targets but also killed civilians. Turkish paratroopers landed near the Nicosia international airport—located in the Greek Cypriot quarter—which each side fought to control.

The junta-controlled Cypriot National Guard and the EOKA B attacked Turkish Cypriot enclaves, such as Limassol, where many hundreds of Turkish Cypriots were held as prisoners. Throughout the island, Greek Cypriot forces murdered hundreds of Turkish Cypriot citizens. The Turkish forces raped and killed men, women, and children and looted homes from which Greek Cypriots fled. The Turks also transported hundreds of Greek Cypriots to prisons in Turkey.

Meanwhile, as fighting raged in Cyprus, a war between Greece and Turkey loomed. Greek troops moved toward the border

UPI/Corbis-Bettmann

Turkish Republic of Northern Cyprus

Above: *Turkish paratroopers dropped from an air force transport plane near Kyrenia on July 20, 1974.* Right: *Turkish soldiers lob grenades during the fighting.*

Shifting Loyalties

After the coup against Makarios, a small number of Greek Cypriots greeted the Turkish troops as liberators from the Greek military dictatorship. Most, however, did not. The threat of attack by Turkey, which was seen as a common enemy, was enough to convince most Greek Cypriots to rally together. The Sampson government emptied the jails of Makarios supporters, many of whom it had slated for death, and rearmed the people it had so recently disarmed. Even though Turkey's stated goal was to topple the new regime and to return Makarios to power, these released prisoners joined the ranks of Greek junta supporters to fight the Turks.

Just a few days before the Turkish attack, Greek Cypriots had held opposing loyalties—supporting either Makarios or the Greek junta. Suddenly the recent enemies were fighting side by side. Greek Cypriots who were not able to change their frame of reference so rapidly continued the enosis argument among themselves. There were some cases reported of Greek Cypriots killing one another while battling the Turks.

Embassy of the Republic of Cyprus

The mangled body of a young Greek Cypriot hangs from the rubble of an apartment building in Famagusta, a target of the Turkish air strike in 1974.

between the two countries, where Turkish troops waited to meet them. The minor shooting incidents that occurred accelerated the UN's efforts to establish peace negotiations. And on July 22, the UN Security Council demanded a cease-fire.

After three days of heavy fighting, the Sampson regime collapsed. Sampson asked Glafkos Clerides, the president of the Greek Cypriot-run House of Representatives, to take over as acting president of the Republic of Cyprus. At almost the same time, the junta—humiliated by its unpreparedness for a full-scale war against Turkey—fell from power in Greece.

Although a UN cease-fire existed officially, fighting continued. Greek Cypriots accused Turkey of trying to expand its hold in Cyprus, and Turkey claimed that it was responding to continued attacks against Turkish Cypriot enclaves.

On July 25, British, Turkish, and Greek officials met

UPI/Corbis-Bettmann

On July 30, 1974, the foreign ministers of Turkey (left), *Britain* (center), *and Greece* (right) *joined in a three-way handshake after signing an agreement to end the fighting in Cyprus.*

in Geneva, Switzerland, to arrange a truce. After days of difficult negotiations, the two sides signed the Geneva Declaration on July 30. Turkey was allowed to keep troops on the island until an "acceptable" settlement could be reached, and it could keep land occupied after the July 22 cease-fire. Greece agreed to halt all aggression against Turkish Cypriots and to withdraw from Turkish Cypriot enclaves. Both sides were to release military and civilian prisoners. The three guarantor powers also agreed to establish a buffer zone that 5,000 UNFICYP troops would patrol.

But even after the second cease-fire, there was scattered fighting. The guarantor powers met again in Geneva on August 10 and were joined by Cypriot representatives Clerides and Denktaş. Denktaş demanded that Cyprus be divided into two ethnic zones, which would be loosely ruled by a central government. He also insisted that Turkish Cypriots needed more than 30 percent of the island to sustain a separate community.

On August 14, Clerides asked for a two-day recess to discuss Turkish Cypriot demands with Makarios in London. But Turkey had lost patience. Greek Cypriot forces still held Turkish Cypriot prisoners in Limassol, Larnaca, and Paphos and still occupied Turkish Cypriot enclaves. Within hours of Clerides's request for a recess, the Turkish army

Anti-American Feelings Set Off Protests

Several times since the 1950s, the U.S. position regarding Cyprus has angered Greeks and Greek Cypriots, leading to violent anti-American demonstrations. In 1954 the United States abstained when the UN voted to decide whether Cypriots had the right to choose their political future. A yes vote would have meant backing for Greek Cypriots, the majority in Cyprus, and therefore for enosis. But the United States refused to vote, because it was torn between support for self-determination and support for continued British rule to stabilize the Mediterranean area. Greece interpreted the U.S. move as support for Britain. Participants at demonstrations in Athens carried banners that read "Americans, we prefer obvious enemies to friends like you."

In 1964, before UN peacekeepers took over, the United States said it was willing to send troops into the newly independent Cyprus to help British forces keep apart the warring ethnic communities. Greek Cypriots gathered at the U.S. Embassy to protest, claiming that the U.S. attitude revealed favoritism toward Turkish Cypriots. Greek Cypriots felt the United States was biased because of NATO's dependence on Turkey's important location.

And just after the Greek junta's coup and the Turkish intervention in 1974, anti-American feelings peaked among Greeks and Greek Cypriots. Protests took place in both Athens and Nicosia. On August 19, Greek Cypriots demonstrated in front of the U.S. Embassy in Nicosia. They charged the United States with not doing enough, including sending U.S. troops, to stop the Turkish advance. Greek Cypriot extremists took advantage of the protest to assassinate U.S. ambassador Rodger Davies. From an apartment building across the street, gunmen opened fire on the embassy with automatic rifles, successfully aiming shots at Davies through an office window.

With Davies's death, the anti-American fury declined. The murder could have severed relations between the United States and the Republic of Cyprus, but various congresspeople and members of the Greek-American population urged the government administration to stay involved in the peace process.

advanced. By August 16, when Turkey agreed to a UN cease-fire, the Turkish army controlled 37 percent of Cyprus, displacing many thousands of northern Cyprus's Greek Cypriots. Greek Cypriot witnesses claim that the TMT also killed many Greek Cypriots during and just after Turkey's second wave of attacks. In the end, Turkish and Turkish Cypriot forces had caused the deaths of thousands of Greek Cypriots.

DIVIDED ISLAND

After the cease-fire, Turkish Cypriots controlled the entire northern coast of Cyprus. The Attila Line zigzagged across the island from Morphou Bay on the western coast to just south of Famagusta on the eastern coast and separated Cyprus into distinct ethnic zones.

About one-third of the Cypriot population had become or would soon become refugees. By September the Greek Cypriot-run government had set up tent camps where some Greek Cypriot refugees stayed. Many had left behind land, homes, thriving businesses, and almost all personal possessions.

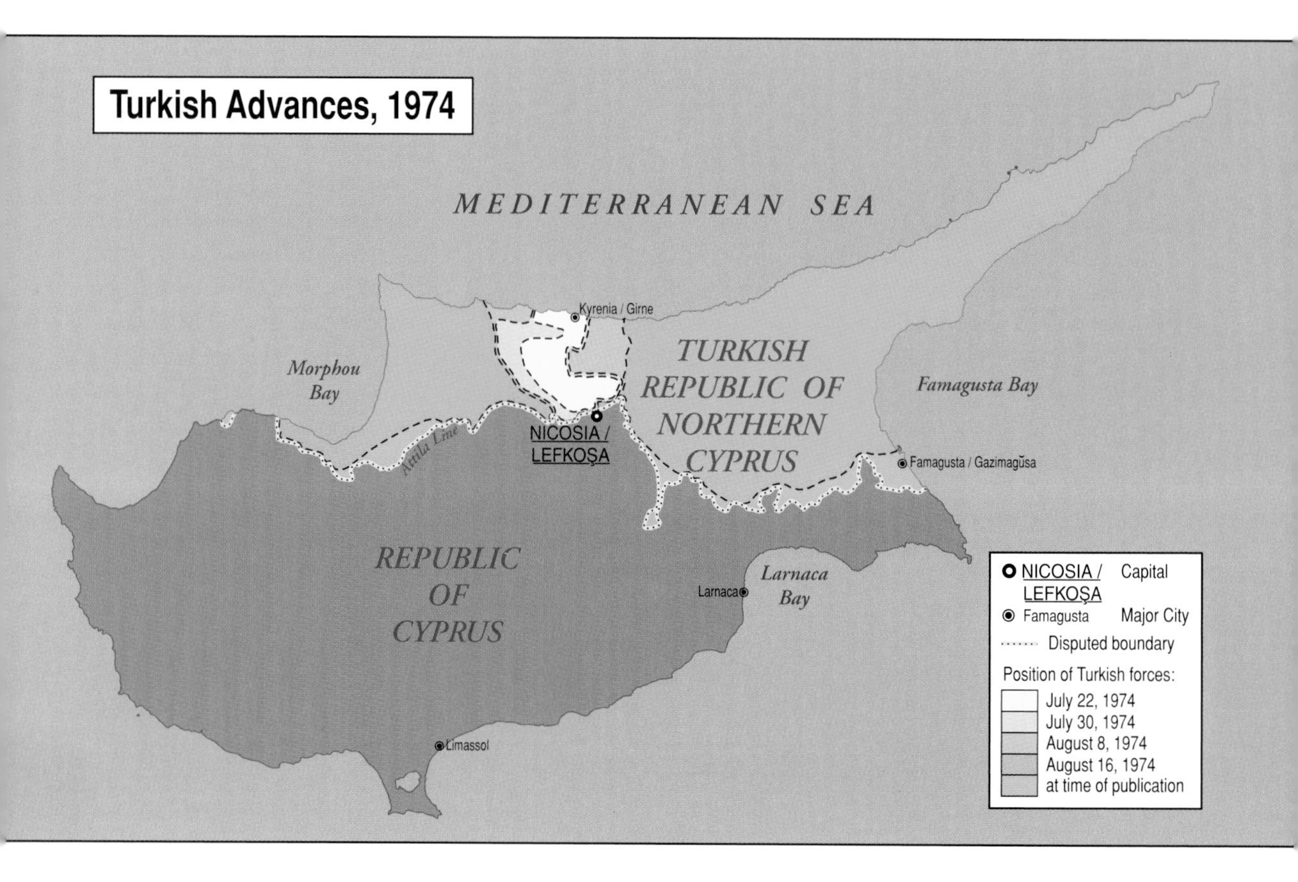

Most expected to return home soon and were anxious for leaders of the ethnic communities to reach an agreement.

Although some Turkish Cypriots had escaped to northern Cyprus during attacks by the National Guard and by the EOKA B, others waited. Turkish Cypriot mass graves uncovered after the cease-fire convinced many Turkish Cypriots still in the south to travel north for safety. Turkish Cypriot leaders accused others who wanted to remain in the Greek Cypriot-controlled area of being traitors, threatening those who were still reluctant to leave. Some poorer Turkish Cypriots were lured north by the prospect of being awarded vacated Greek Cypriot homes, fields, and fruit orchards. Meanwhile, thousands of Turkish troops and their families were invited to settle permanently in the northern zone. Many settlers from Turkey also were given Greek Cypriot property, which the Turkish Cypriot government said had been abandoned.

In the months following the summer fighting, discussions regarding humanitarian issues began between Clerides and Denktaş. Makarios resumed presidential duties upon his return to Cyprus in December 1974, but Clerides continued his role as the Greek Cypriot representative in intercommunal negotiations. Although much of the Cypriot population transfer occurred during or shortly after the summer's fighting, a voluntary population exchange was agreed upon in August 1975. Shortly after plans for the population exchange were reached, thousands more refugees from both ethnic communities crossed the Attila Line to begin new lives outside their home territories.

After the end of this large-scale population transfer, the Attila Line became nearly impossible to penetrate. The United Nations moved its thousands of peacekeepers between the two hostile armies. Roadblocks strictly regulated passage between zones. UN forces observed from watchtowers set up along the buffer zone.

OFF-AND-ON TALKS

Early negotiations between Cypriot ethnic communities focused on several questions. These questions included the type of constitutional arrangement that should govern Cyprus; resolution of territorial questions and the refugee situation; and timing for the withdrawal of Turkish troops.

In 1975, foreseeing that diplomatic talks may be drawn out, the leaders of the Turkish Cypriot Provisional Administration founded the Turkish Federated State of Cyprus (TFSC). They did not attempt to gain international recognition as an independent state because they intended to continue negotiations with Greek Cypriots to achieve a federal solution. In the meantime, Denktaş wanted to provide the Turkish Cypriot community with better government services than the provisional administration could furnish.

Turkish Cypriots and Greek Cypriots quickly agreed upon two points.

Claude Salhani/Sygma

Crowds of Greek Cypriots, some carrying a huge image of Makarios, greeted the president's return in December of 1974.

M. Ergün Olgun

Rauf Denktaş came into the political limelight in the 1960s as the Turkish Cypriot representative in intercommunal talks. Since then he has steadfastly negotiated for a segregated federation in Cyprus in which the ethnic communities would be united under a single central government but in which each would have its own self-ruling territory. Denktaş's announcement in 1983 of the formation of the TRNC underscored his desire to maintain the equality of Turkish Cypriot citizens.

Cyprus should remain an independent country and should be demilitarized. Denktaş advocated a bizonal federation, by which he meant the two ethnic communities would unite under one constitution but would remain largely segregated. Although Clerides appeared willing to accept this proposal, Makarios did not. Clerides resigned as chief Greek Cypriot negotiator.

The picture brightened a bit in early 1977 when Makarios and Denktaş conducted talks in Vienna under UN guidance. By this time, Makarios had shifted his position. The leaders agreed that Cyprus should be a bicommunal, bizonal federation that was independent and not aligned with other countries. They also agreed that the land under each ethnic community's administration must be sufficient in size and resources to support the community. Other issues—such as freedom of movement, of settlement, and of property ownership—were "open for discussion."

Although the Vienna agreements laid down an important foundation for later negotiations, the negotiators had very different visions of a federation. Makarios wanted a strong central government with limited sovereignty of each state. Denktaş advocated a weaker central government with each state having extensive administrative freedom. Makarios died in August 1977 before further progress could be made. The Greek Cypriot vice president Spyros Kyprianou took over the office of president.

Under pressure from Greek Cypriot refugees, Kyprianou insisted on the refugees' right to move back to northern Cyprus. He also tried to isolate the Turkish Cypriots through an embargo and called for the removal of Turkish troops. Also blocking the negotiations was each ethnic community's perception of fair representation in the federal government. Turkish Cypriots viewed the proposed federation to be made of two states that would have equal status and representation. Greek Cypriots wanted proportional representation. That is, the number of representatives would reflect the percentage each group represented within the total Cypriot population. Under this system, Greek Cypriots would have a majority.

In May 1983, the UN General Assembly voted that Turkey should remove its troops from Cyprus. In response Denktaş threatened to forego intercommunal negotiations and declared the independence of the Turkish-controlled zone, as the Turkish Republic of Northern Cyprus (TRNC). This state gained formal recognition only from Turkey.

The international community saw this step as an affront to conflict resolution efforts. Denktaş defended his decision, stating that his intention was to stimulate negotiations, not to block a federal solution. By declaring independence, Denktaş claimed, the Turkish Cypriot community acquired a political identity. As citizens of an independent state, Turkish Cypriots stood a chance of being perceived as an equal negotiator rather than as a Cypriot minority.

In January 1985, Denktaş and Kyprianou met to discuss a UN plan. At first the response of both leaders was positive, and UN negotiators were optimistic that a settlement was near. Denktaş agreed to sign a draft of the plan, noting that details would need to be hammered out later. Kyprianou, however, surprised external observers when he reversed his initial enthusiasm and refused to sign the draft. Observers speculated that pressure from the Greek government caused his about-face. The UN team revised the draft several times to make it acceptable to both sides, but with each new revision one side or the other was unwilling to commit.

In November 1983, after the announcement of the formation of the TRNC, the U.S. State Department replied, "We are dismayed by the move. . . . We will not recognize the new polity, and we urge all countries of the world not to recognize it."

Intercommunal leaders did not meet again until August 1988, when George Vassiliou, the newly elected president of the Republic of Cyprus, sat down with Denktaş in Geneva. After some initial attempts to compromise, both sides backed off. Talks collapsed completely in early 1990 because Denktaş demanded the right of self-determination for Turkish Cypriots.

In July 1990, the Republic of Cyprus applied to join the European Community (EC, which in 1993 was renamed the EU). This action angered Denktaş because the Greek Cypriot president had not consulted Turkish Cypriots. That same month, Denktaş signed an agreement with Turkey's prime minister, linking more closely the economies of the TRNC and Turkey.

With little progress toward settlement being made, the two Cypriot communities began to look elsewhere for solutions. Greek Cypriot leaders, for example, increased their efforts to internationalize the issue. The Republic of Cyprus asked other nations to use Turkey's EC application to pressure Turkey to remove its troops. Greek Cypriot leaders also wanted Turkey to convince Turkish Cypriots to be more flexible at the negotiating table. Meanwhile, the Turkish Cypriot administration began pushing for wider recognition of the TRNC.

By the early 1990s, UN resources and international attention were stretched thin by the outbreak of conflict in the Middle East, where Iraq had invaded Kuwait. Not until early 1991 did Cyprus return to the agenda of international policymakers. In that year, attempts by the EU, the UN, and U.S. president George Bush failed to gather Cypriot, Turkish, and Greek leaders for a proposed conference.

But in 1992, the UN's new secretary-general, Boutros Boutros-Ghali, held private meetings with each Cypriot leader that eventually brought Vassiliou and Denktaş face to face. Boutros-Ghali had developed a "set of ideas," based on points of agreement that had been reached over years of negotiations. By using this document, UN leaders hoped Cyprus's leaders could draw up a draft settlement. Vassiliou accepted the document with certain provisions. Denktaş rejected the UN's proposed division of territory and other aspects of the "set of ideas," which he said did not discuss many fundamental concerns of Turkish Cypriots. Once again, talks ended without progress.

By November 1992, a solution to the Cyprus situation seemed farther away than ever. According to Boutros-Ghali, there was a "deep crisis of confidence between the two sides." To promote trust, the UN recommended taking confidence-building measures (CBMs), steps that included incentives for both Cypriot governments to cooperate with the peacemaking process.

One important proposal was the reopening of the Nicosia international airport, which has been closed since 1974. Opening the airport

AP/Wide World Photos

Talks about settling the Cyprus question have long involved the United Nations. In January 1993, the organization's then secretary-general, Boutros Boutros-Ghali (right), *shook hands with the then president of the Republic of Cyprus, George Vassiliou, before a round of meetings in France.*

North of the UN outpost at Dherinia is the abandoned resort town of Varosha, where the Republic of Cyprus wants to resettle 35,000 Greek Cypriots.

would give the TRNC links to the international community. An important accommodation for Greek Cypriots was the suggested open zone in Varosha, formerly a popular seaside resort on Cyprus's eastern coast. Tens of thousands of Greek Cypriots had abandoned Varosha when it came under Turkish attack in 1974. The town had never been reoccupied. Boutros-Ghali proposed that Varosha become a small free-trade zone, with Greek Cypriots and Turkish Cypriots allowed to come and go as they pleased. Other CBMs included the reduction of the number of Turkish troops and the promotion of contact between Greek Cypriot and Turkish Cypriot citizens.

A new Republic of Cyprus president, Glafkos Clerides, who narrowly won the election in February 1993, met with Denktaş in New York in May to discuss the CBMs. Denktaş added to the CBMs the demand that the Republic of Cyprus lift the embargo against TRNC ports and airports. By June talks had stalled when Denktaş would not respond to the proposed UN CBMs. In late 1993, the EU appointed an observer to monitor negotiations when UN talks resumed. Meanwhile, the governments of Greece and the Republic of Cyprus announced they would make joint decisions regarding a Cyprus settlement. The two countries also entered into a common defense pact in which Greece guaranteed

Embassy of the Republic of Cyprus

As direct talks stalled between the two Cypriot leaders, the United States sent Richard Beattie (right) *to try to restart them. Here he meets with Glafkos Clerides, the president of the Republic of Cyprus.*

military protection to its ethnic kin in Cyprus.

In early 1994, both sides agreed in principle to the CBMs, and the UN began separate negotiations with Clerides and Denktaş for implementing them. But Denktaş soon accused the UN of changing the proposals, and talks stalled. In June Denktaş submitted some clarifications, which—if inserted into the CBM document—would make it acceptable to the Turkish Cypriot government. Clerides told the UN that he would not negotiate on changes to the CBMs he had already agreed to accept.

In July 1994, the EU Court of Justice ruled that its member-countries couldn't continue to purchase TRNC produce, motivating Denktaş to state that a Cypriot federation was no longer an option. The TRNC, Denktaş threatened, would establish closer ties to Turkey. Adding to Denktaş's determination was the EU's decision to allow the Republic of Cyprus to join the organization during its next round of expansion. (The EU did tie the membership process to the progress of settlement talks.) In October 1994, Clerides and Denktaş met with UN officials in several face-to-face meetings. Each leader stood firm in his demands. Clerides said he would refuse to continue talks until the Turkish Cypriot leader accepted the EU application. Denktaş stated his resolve to oppose the application until a settlement for Cyprus had been reached.

Both leaders took strong stances and direct contact between them ended, but each Cypriot leader publicly supported peace talks. Under the guidance of the United States and Britain, low-level negotiations took place in May 1995 but made little progress.

Although Denktaş and Clerides had stopped talking to one another, other governments and international organizations were becoming more involved. The EU voted to accept the Republic of Cyprus regardless of the status of a settlement. On a trip to Cyprus in late 1995, U.S. presidential emissary Richard Beattie in conjunction with Turkish Cypriot leaders drew up proposals that aimed to restart direct talks. Clerides rejected these proposals, saying the Turkish Cypriot side had nothing new to offer.

In early 1996, the European Court of Human Rights tried a case filed against Turkey by Titina Loizidou, a Greek Cypriot refugee. The court found Turkey guilty of violating Loizidou's right to enjoy her property in northern Cyprus since the military intervention in the summer of 1974.

International concern about Cyprus's potential as a military hotspot soared in 1996. Tensions between Greece and Turkey over territorial issues in the Aegean Sea resurfaced. In August the plans for the Greek Cypriot-sponsored motorcycle rally to cross into the TRNC triggered the worst violence in Cyprus since the island's division and strong nationalist reactions by both Greece and Turkey. In January 1997, the Republic of Cyprus, with backing from Greece, agreed to purchase a highly sophisticated, Russian-made, long-range defense missile system. Turkey responded that it would "take necessary measures" to stop Greece and Greek Cypriots from upsetting the region's military balance. Cypriots and the rest of the world are waiting to see what will happen next. 🌐

AP/Wide World Photos

A Turkish soldier watches the UN buffer zone that lies beyond the flags of the TRNC (left) *and Turkey.*

CHAPTER 5

WHAT'S BEING DONE TO SOLVE THE PROBLEM

On July 9, 1997, after a thirty-two-month break in negotiations, UN efforts again brought together Clerides and Denktaş for direct talks in New York. Clerides stated that his intention is to reach an overall settlement, which he warned must be based on international law as well as on the UN and the EU charters for human rights. In preparation for intercommunal negotiations, he had flown to Athens, where he and Greek officials developed a joint position on "safety limits" for the talks. Meanwhile, Denktaş assured the international community of his desire for a resolution resulting from the face-to-face meetings.

According to Kofi Annan, who was elected UN secretary-general in 1996, the organization is determined that Cypriot leaders continue discussions "as long as may be needed to achieve agreement on a comprehensive settlement." To bolster UN negotiations, the United States assigned Richard Holbrooke, former assistant secretary of state, as a special presidential envoy to conduct talks that parallel the UN negotiations.

Turkish Republic of Northern Cyprus

As in the past, the UN, the United States, and the EU support the aim of an independent bicommunal, bizonal federation in Cyprus.

UN TALKS

Attending negotiations in July along with Clerides, Denktaş, and UN representatives were diplomats from Greece, Turkey, Britain, and the United States. At Greece's request, EU observers sat in on the meetings. Both Cypriot leaders expressed the fear that if a settlement isn't found Cyprus "might be destroyed." Yet the same issues that have plagued past negotiations are still challenging community leaders. These issues include refugee and territorial matters, the settler question, demilitarization of the island, protecting the new federation, and the amount of control bestowed on a central government. A comprehensive settlement will require both ethnic communities to compromise.

Although the two community leaders acknowledge that reaching a political solution will require give and take, each stood firm on two issues. Clerides expects Turkey to show its goodwill by following UN and U.S. resolutions that call for demilitarization in Cyprus. Denktaş insists Turkish troops must remain in place until a settlement is achieved that guarantees the status of Turkish Cypriots.

According to Clerides, Denktaş's concern about Turkish Cypriots' rights and safety is unfounded and will be even more so when Cyprus belongs to the EU. Denktaş claims that EU membership before settlement will eliminate Greek Cypriot incentive to resolve the division between communities. He warns that Cyprus's membership talks must not begin until after Greek Cypriots and Turkish Cypriots have reached a political solution. The Republic of Cyprus remains determined to go ahead with EU **accession** talks. However, to help Denktaş come to terms with its position, Clerides has invited Turkish

The Enclaved

Citizens who chose to remain in their homes on the "wrong" side of the buffer zone after government leaders signed a population exchange in 1975 became known as the "enclaved." The number of enclaved Greek Cypriots and Turkish Cypriots has continued to decline because of the harassment and economic difficulties they've experienced from living apart from their ethnic kin. Approximately 9,000 Greek Cypriot citizens had stayed in the north, but these days the number is less than 500. The number of Turkish Cypriots enclaved in southern Cyprus is also about 500, concentrated mostly in Limassol. On both sides of the Attila Line, the government in charge keeps close tabs on the enclaved, who are often accused of being spies for the other government.

Facing page: *During another round of face-to-face negotiations, Gustave Feissel, representing the UN, stood between Glafkos Clerides* (front left) *and Rauf Denktaş* (front right).

Cypriot trade unions and chambers of commerce to be involved in the island's EU negotiations. In addition, Clerides said, if a settlement is reached, the Republic of Cyprus would have no reason to deploy the Russian-made anti-aircraft missile defense system that's scheduled for delivery in mid-1998.

The main goal for the first round of UN talks was for Clerides and Denktaş to agree on boundaries for the negotiations, saving work on the actual substance of issues for later. Before they left New York, Clerides and Denktaş committed to continue UN talks and to meet informally in Nicosia to discuss humanitarian issues

Sovfoto/Itar-Tass

The Republic of Cyprus has ordered a Russian-made missile system.

The Missing

Even with Cypriot leaders issuing escalating threats, positive progress did occur after the UN-sponsored negotiations in July 1997. Clerides and Denktaş agreed to take immediate steps to determine the fate of more than 2,000 Greek Cypriots and Turkish Cypriots who had disappeared from 1964 to 1974. The two governments simultaneously will exchange any information they have regarding the location of graves—mass and individual—in which the missing might be buried. The bodies will be taken out of their graves, scientifically identified, and then the remains will be returned to the families for proper burial. The governments also will return the bodies of those known to have been killed in action.

prior to the next official round. At the same time, though, the EU reaffirmed that Cyprus would begin membership talks in early 1998, while Turkey would not.

The international response to the EU decision was favorable, and the EU, Greece, the UN, and the United States want intercommunal negotiations and EU accession talks to take place at the same time. They believe the Republic of Cyprus's bid for membership provides a catalyst for settlement talks.

Turkey and Turkish Cypriots, however, reacted strongly to the EU decision. Denktaş threatened to quit the talks if Turkey wasn't approved for EU membership and if the EU went ahead with Cyprus's accession process. The Turkish deputy prime minister Bülent Ecevit said the EU decision made the "partial integration" of the TRNC and Turkey inevitable. Under an integration agreement signed on August 6, the people of the TRNC and Turkey would have dual citizenship, and Turkey would handle economic, defense, and foreign policy for both.

Homeland Relations

The rivalry between Greece and Turkey has long cast a shadow over Cyprus. Because each ethnic community in Cyprus has strong cultural ties its homeland, increasing tensions between Greece and Turkey often have translated into rising pressures on the island. The troubles in Cyprus have likewise brought the homelands close to war several times.

A promising turn in Greek-Turkish relations corresponded with the UN-sponsored intercommunal negotiations between Clerides and Denktaş in July of 1997. In the days before the Cypriot leaders met, Greece and Turkey signed a nonaggression pact at a NATO summit in Madrid, Spain. The NATO allies agreed to resolve their conflict over which country holds the rights to a potentially oil-rich area in the Aegean Sea through diplomacy rather than through violence. This question and that of ownership of uninhabited islands near the Turkish coast have been the key issues unsettling relations between the countries.

Greece and Turkey entered into the Madrid agreement partly to promote their respective interests in the next wave of EU expansion, a process that is scheduled to begin in early 1998. Greece wanted to help the Republic of Cyprus's bid for membership. Turkey wanted to move from a customs union to full membership—a change to which Greece objects.

As Denktaş and Clerides were finishing their initial discussions, the EU reaffirmed its decision to allow Cyprus to begin accession talks. The organization meanwhile denied Turkey that opportunity. This announcement led Turkey and the TRNC to sign a partial integration agreement. Greece views closer ties between Turks and Turkish Cypriots as a threat to Greek Cypriots.

Once again the homelands are threatening to use force to settle differences in Cyprus. Greece and Turkey have taken opposite sides regarding the Republic of Cyprus's plans for purchasing a long-range, anti-aircraft missile system from Russia. Turkish officials, who see the Greek Cypriot arms buildup as an offensive military operation, claim they will attack if the missile system is put into place. Greek leaders, stating the missile system is necessary for Greek Cypriot defense, threaten to attack Turkey if Turkey interferes with the installation.

Embassy of the Republic of Cyprus

As the UN's Diego Cordovez (center) *looked on, Clerides and Denktaş shook hands at the start of their August 1997 meetings in Switzerland. The two sides made little progress. As a result, Cordovez set up the next round of talks for 1998, after the Republic of Cyprus will have held presidential elections and after the EU will have initiated membership discussions.*

Calling the move toward partial integration blackmail, Clerides upped the stakes. If settlement talks did not continue, he stated, the Republic of Cyprus would go ahead with its plans to install the Russian-made anti-aircraft missile system. Turkey topped the Greek Cypriot threat with one of its own: If missiles were deployed, Turkey would attack them.

Despite Denktaş's threats to the contrary, he met with Clerides on August 11 in Glion-sur-Montreux, Switzerland, to continue UN-sponsored talks. His decision may have been due in part to the insistence of Turkish Cypriot opposition party leaders.

The UN's aim was for Clerides and Denktaş to reach a jointly held position on how to proceed to a comprehensive settlement. The UN asked each side to submit a draft constitution by the end of the year so that work on actual legal documents for the federation could begin in 1998. But at the close of the second round of talks, the Cypriot communities hadn't reached an agreed-upon path for future negotiations. Denktaş said he would not negotiate until the Republic of Cyprus agreed to withdraw its EU application or until the EU reversed its decision to proceed with accession talks. The Republic of Cyprus refused to take back its application.

UN head negotiator Diego Cordovez delayed the next talks until March 1998, after the Republic of Cyprus has held presidential elections and after EU accession talks, if started as scheduled, are under way. These events will strongly impact future UN negotiations.

Institute for Multi-Track Diplomacy

During a training session, Cypriot participants learn to negotiate. Without coaching on effective communication techniques, Turkish Cypriots and Greek Cypriots alike try to explain "the truth" to the other side. This approach meets resistance, and discussions often break down. The training helps Cypriots overcome these difficulties so that communication can succeed.

CITIZEN PEACEMAKERS

Alongside the UN-sponsored negotiations are the ongoing efforts of many groups and individuals in Cyprus and abroad. A growing number of citizens in the two communities are dedicated to rebuilding trust and lines of communication. These peacemakers believe that if Greek Cypriots and Turkish Cypriots don't change their long-standing attitudes toward one another before a political settlement is reached, a Cyprus federation is likely to fail.

In 1993 the Institute for Multi-Track Diplomacy

Institute for Multi-Track Diplomacy

Many of the bicommunal meetings take place in the UN buffer zone, where each side is free of harassment and propaganda.

(IMTD), the Conflict Management Group, and the NTL Institute for Applied Behavioral Sciences formed the Cyprus Consortium. This U.S.-based umbrella organization has stimulated and guided citizen interest in peacebuilding activities. The Consortium holds conflict-resolution training sessions for Greek Cypriots and Turkish Cypriots, often in the United States. After going back to Cyprus, these trainees, in turn, become trainers of other people interested in reestablishing relations between communities. IMTD wants to create a network of citizen peacebuilders—Greek Cypriot and Turkish Cypriot policymakers, businesspersons, educators, and ordinary citizens—who have the skills necessary for improving intercommunal relations. Once the network is in place, these individuals will work to help transform their society.

At first many people in Cyprus didn't trust their Consortium-trained community members. Some factions went so far as to threaten or harm the peacebuilders. But in just a few years, the peacebuilders have earned the respect of many Greek Cypriots and Turkish Cypriots and are struggling to meet the growing demand for training.

Consortium-trained peacebuilders organize both ongoing bicommunal groups and one-time events, such as a UN Day celebration in the buffer zone just a few weeks after the violence in August 1996. They have enabled Greek Cypriots and Turkish Cypriots to write columns for newspapers across the buffer zone. The peacebuilders seek publishers for bicommunal books of poetry and short stories.

Institute for Multi-Track Diplomacy

Consortium-trained Cypriots organized a UN Day celebration in the buffer zone on October 24, 1996, that attracted nearly 3,000 Cypriots in support of peace and reconciliation. Many attendees asked how they could get more involved in bicommunal activities.

Website Wizard

The Internet may help shape Cyprus's future. Electronic communication has made it easy for Cypriot students studying abroad to "cross the line." Lists of e-mail addresses let Greek Cypriot and Turkish Cypriot students contact one another for electronic discussions. If students happen to attend the same university or one nearby, they may meet in person.

Internet information about the Cyprus conflict varies tremendously. Some sites present nationalist viewpoints similar to the one-sided attitudes that fill most of the island's news sources. Many Cypriot students have had enough of finger-pointing and are looking for constructive avenues of communication. Turgut Durduran—a Turkish Cypriot studying at the University of Pennsylvania—maintains a bicommunal website with many of his own pages, as well as links to other sites. Included online is the bicommunal journal *Crossings,* which he and Greek Cypriot Anthony Koyzis cofounded. Hundreds of thousands of visitors have logged on to Durduran's site at http://www.stwing.upenn.edu/~durduran/cyprus1.html. Among his many other reconciliation activities, Turgut is involved in expanding Cypriots' access to the Internet in Cyprus, and he plans to help set up a bicommunal server.

Turgut Durduran

Rather than waiting for Cypriot leaders to solve the tensions between the island's ethnic communities, Turkish Cypriot Turgut Durduran encourages individuals to become involved. Turgut's website posts bicommunal activities and groups, as well as e-mail addresses for Cypriots who want to participate in electronic intercommunal chats.

Turgut's parents probably sparked his strong peacemaking interests. In 1976 Turgut's father, Alpay Durduran, founded the Communal Liberation Party. In 1989 he established the New Cyprus Party (NCP), which promotes Cyprus's speedy entry into the EU. The NCP also favors a federation that respects human rights and international law. Sefika Durduran—Turgut's mother—belongs to the bicommunal Lawyers Group. She is also involved in Cyprus Link, a bicommunal women's organization that plans to replace history books perpetuating nationalist attitudes. The group also pushes for increased tolerance and encourages Cypriots to learn the other ethnic community's language as well as English.

Promoting bicommunal relations requires courage and persistence. Turgut says extremists make constant threats. Both the NCP headquarters and the Durduran home have been attacked with bombs and machine guns.

All of the Consortium-trained groups in Cyprus meet in the buffer zone, which these days is the only available place for bicommunal activity. Among the most active organizations is the European Union–Federation Study Group. Its goal is to inform citizens from both communities of the advantages, difficulties, and concerns of joining the EU. The group has invited high-ranking EU members to present information about policies, institutions, and funding.

The Educators Group compared the Greek Cypriot and Turkish Cypriot educational systems and set up projects within the schools to advance peacemaking. The group undertook a "letter to the other side," which gave children the opportunity to share their culture and viewpoints with one another.

Membership in the Citizens Group keeps growing. These Turkish Cypriots and Greek Cypriots have developed a shared vision of how they can contribute to peace in Cyprus.

The Youth Leaders Group is addressing the great challenges facing Cyprus's young people, whom the Consortium believes will play an important role in the peacemaking movement. Cyprus's teenagers don't have memories of intercommunal violence, and almost none have met members from the other ethnic community. Yet the experiences of their older relatives and biased history books and media have colored their perceptions. Nevertheless, many young people in Cyprus have a strong desire to meet their counterparts across the buffer zone and to discover for themselves what they are like.

Plans for a New Nicosia

In Cyprus common work projects have offered a way for Greek Cypriots and Turkish Cypriots to reestablish relationships. Under UN direction, workers from the two communities have repaired water systems and electricity lines along the buffer zone. Plans for rebuilding neighborhoods in the capital are on the drawing board.

The division of Nicosia has nearly destroyed many of the capital's oldest neighborhoods. Homes have been abandoned, and streets and sidewalks have deteriorated. Healing the historic inner neighborhoods has become an important bicommunal dream—one that only can be realized when the buffer zone disappears. In 1979 Lellos Demetriades and Mustafa Akinci began working on the Nicosia Master Plan. Teams of Greek Cypriot and Turkish Cypriot planners, engineers, and architects have met in the buffer zone and have worked together on the blueprints, which prepare for the city's future as an undivided capital of Cyprus.

The Nicosia Master Plan includes many different projects. Crews will rebuild the old neighborhoods of Chrysaliniotissa and Arab Ahmet, which lie on opposite sides of the buffer zone. Workers will repair houses and sidewalks, as well as the sixteenth-century wall and moats that surround the city. The plans also include the creation of new public markets, parks, community centers, and an open-air theater. If these projects go forward, Nicosia may again prosper from the cooperative efforts of the two ethnic communities.

In July 1997, the Cyprus Consortium brought together 40 teenagers—20 Greek Cypriots and 20 Turkish Cypriots—to attend a two-week camp in Waynesboro, Pennsylvania. At camp they shared meals, living quarters, work projects, and leisure time.

The Consortium's goals for the youth camp were much the same as its goals in working with Cyprus's adults—to promote cross-cultural tolerance; to replace stereotypes; to advance trust and respect; to increase leadership capacity; and to develop conflict-resolution skills.

Most mornings in camp, the teens participated in conflict-resolution training sessions. The teens first examined their own beliefs and then shared their impressions of the other community. They also compared the history they had learned and realized that the past is often much more complex than how it has been portrayed. The campers moved quickly from defending their version of history to asking teens from the other community for help in expanding their viewpoint. This openness allowed the teens to move on to developing bicommunal goals.

The Nicosia Master Plan intends to renovate dilapidated areas of the capital.

The Greek Cypriot and Turkish Cypriot teenagers deepened their new relationships by participating in sporting events, talent shows, evenings around the campfire, and sightseeing trips. On the last night, the campers held a candle-lighting ritual, during which they expressed sadness that their budding friendships would be difficult to maintain in a divided Cyprus. Equipped with new communication skills, they returned to the island eager to share their bicommunal experience with others. Their goal is to encourage more people, especially their peers, to participate in bicommunal activities.

AMIDEAST

AMIDEAST

During a confidence-building workshop held in the United States, CASP university students from both Cypriot communities participated in a ropes course (right) *to test and foster trust. Leisure time around the campfire* (left) *also strengthened understanding and dispelled prejudices.*

Institute for Multi-Track Diplomacy

Other peacemaking organizations also work to shift young Cypriots' attitudes about the other community. The Cyprus-America Scholarship Program (CASP), administered by AMIDEAST, sponsors more than 170 Greek Cypriots and Turkish Cypriots to study in the United States. In 1996 and 1997, before heading to their respective universities for fall classes, some of CASP's second- and third-year students got together for a week-long confidence-building workshop. Run by the School for International Training in Brattleboro, Vermont, these workshops guided attendees from the two communities as they compared upbringings and beliefs. The students found that centuries of geographic proximity had created many more shared traditions than the media in Cyprus portrays. The students dispelled cultural stereotypes by sharing information about their lives and beliefs and by asking and answering questions.

These young adults feel that attending school abroad has enabled them to accept one another as individuals. For the male students in particular, this is a large step. By the time most of these young Greek Cypriot and Turkish Cypriot men begin college, they have already completed two years of compulsory military service. While in the army, they were trained to see those from the other ethnic community as the enemy.

Off the island, students get away from the relentless presentation of stereotypes that wedges apart the communities. Yet these students also admit to sometimes slipping back into feeling that it's "us against them" during summer break, when they are once again surrounded by prejudices. To overcome the influence of propaganda, these students have pledged to keep in contact with one another and to participate in peacemaking activities in Cyprus. During the school year, they'll maintain a strong e-mail network.

Until a political settlement is reached—and until more Cypriots are willing to enter into a new relationship with those in the other ethnic community—the island will continue to resemble a small stage on which two very different dramas are being played out. In one drama, growing numbers of Cypriots work to tear down stereotypes and to rebuild trust. Expressing her belief in Cyprus's united future, Gloria, a Cypriot teen, says, "It is in the nature of barriers that they should fall. But sometimes they need a little push." In the other drama, Greek Cypriot soldiers and Turkish and Turkish Cypriot forces watch one another across a strip of empty land with large stocks of weapons at the ready. 🌐

It is in the nature of barriers that they should fall. But sometimes they need a little push.

Facing page: *At the Cyprus Consortium's youth leadership camp, two Greek Cypriot teenagers act out a "reentry" experience in which a U.S.-educated student returns to Cyprus, where he is challenged by a friend to defend his bicommunal views.*

EPILOGUE*

By the fall of 1997, the major issues for Greek Cypriots and Turkish Cypriots had not changed. Tensions still revolve around the upcoming EU accession talks, which are expected to begin in the spring of 1998, and the Russian anti-aircraft missile system that the Republic of Cyprus plans to install that summer. Neither side has changed its stance. To get beyond this impasse, U.S. presidential emissary Richard Holbrooke has asked that Turkish Cypriots participate in the accession talks. Turkish Cypriot participation is an option, according to Denktaş, only if the TRNC is recognized as a political equal and if Turkey is given "privileged country" status in the EU. Meanwhile, Greek Cypriots and Greeks continue to use Turkey's threat to annex northern Cyprus to justify their commitment to military buildup in the Republic of Cyprus. Greece and Russia have threatened war if Turkey attacks ships delivering the missiles.

As political leaders traded threats, Greek, Greek Cypriot, Turkish, and Turkish Cypriot troops—using live ammunition—participated in military exercises on the island. The UN-sponsored intercommunal talks that ended in August 1997 are scheduled to resume in February 1998. In the meantime, Denktaş and Clerides are meeting with international representatives to rally support for their views. Untangling the arguments of the Cypriot leaders remains high on the agenda of international diplomats worldwide. Cypriots hold out hope that political solutions will win out over military options for which both communities are amply prepared.

*Please note: The information presented in *Cyprus: Divided Island* was current at the time of the book's publication. For late-breaking news on the conflict, look for articles in the international section of U.S. daily newspapers. The *Economist*, a weekly magazine, is another good source for up-to-date information. You may also wish to access the following Internet websites: the Republic of Cyprus Press and Information Office at http://www.pio.gov.cy; the Office of the Representative of the TRNC in Washington, D.C., at http://www.trncwashdc.org; the U.S. State Department at http://www.state.gov; and the United Nations at http://www.un.org.

CHRONOLOGY

ca. 1200 B.C. Greeks settle in Cyprus, establishing city-states and bringing Greek culture.

A.D. 45 The apostle Paul arrives in Cyprus and converts islanders from ancient Greek cults to Christianity.

A.D. 488 Greek Cypriots establish the independent Church of Cyprus. At this time, Cyprus is part of the Byzantine Empire, a Greek-speaking, Orthodox Christian empire.

1191 The Church of Cyprus loses influence when Cyprus is governed by a series of European rulers.

1571 Cyprus is conquered by Ottoman Turks. Under this Muslim empire's rule, the Church of Cyprus resumes its former influence. Turkish Cypriot culture is established.

ca. 1830 Greek Cypriots advocate throwing off Ottoman rule and uniting with Greece (enosis).

1878 Turkey leases Cyprus to Britain in exchange for protection from Russia.

1903 British and Turkish Cypriot legislative members vote down Greek Cypriot call for enosis.

1914 Britain takes over Cyprus when Ottomans side with Germany in World War I (1914–1918).

1931 Greek Cypriots violently revolt against tax increase. Britain declares a state of emergency.

1939 World War II begins. Cypriots fight alongside British. When war ends in 1945, Greek Cypriots expect their contribution to be rewarded with self-rule.

1950 Makarios III becomes archbishop. A vote shows that 96 percent of Greek Cypriots desire enosis.

1954 Greece asks the United Nations (UN) to support Cypriots' right to self-determination. Turkish Cypriots ask for partition. The UN decision not to rule inflames Greek Cypriots to riot.

1955 The National Organization of Cypriot Fighters (EOKA), led by Georgios Grivas, begins a guerrilla campaign to overthrow British rule.

1956 Talks between Britain and Makarios about independence break down in March. Makarios is exiled. British leaders develop a proposal that safeguards the rights of Turkish Cypriots.

1957 Turkish Cypriots with Turkish support form the Turkish Resistance Organization (TMT) to resist enosis.

1958 Greece and Turkey begin negotiations for Cyprus's future with independence as the goal.

1959 Greek, Turkish, British, Greek Cypriot, and Turkish Cypriot representatives sign the Zurich-London Agreements that outlaws both enosis and partition. Makarios returns to Cyprus, and Grivas leaves the island.

1960 On August 16, Cyprus becomes an independent republic with Archbishop Makarios as its first president and Fazil Küçük as vice president.

1961 President Makarios establishes a pro-enosis secret army, which Greece helps to supply.

1963 Greek Cypriot leaders circulate the top-secret Akritas Plan, the ultimate goal of which is enosis. On November 30, Makarios presents to Küçük amendments that would diminish Turkish Cypriot rights. On December 21, fighting erupts in Nicosia and spreads throughout the island. Turkey threatens to attack, and Makarios allows Britain to establish a peacekeeping force.

1964 Turkish Cypriots flee to enclaves. British forces establish the Green Line in Nicosia. Joint rule in Cyprus ends. UN peacekeepers replace British forces. Greece agrees to send weapons and troops to Makarios, who is setting up the Cyprus National Guard. Greece sends Grivas to Cyprus to head the Greek army and the National Guard. In early August, National Guard attacks against Turkish Cypriots prompt Turkey to strike. On August 9, Greek Cypriots accept UN cease-fire demands. Makarios supports an economic embargo against Turkish Cypriots.

1967 In April a Greek military junta overthrows the elected Greek government. Grivas orders attacks on Turkish Cypriot enclaves despite Makarios's orders to quit. In autumn tension between Greece and Turkey soars because of Cyprus, but the North Atlantic Treaty Organization (NATO) defuses a war between the member-countries. Turkey issues an ultimatum, and the junta recalls Grivas from Cyprus. Turkish Cypriots set up the Provisional Turkish Cypriot Administration.

1971 Backed by the Greek junta, Grivas secretly returns to Cyprus. He founds a new guerrilla group known as the EOKA B to oust Makarios.

1974 Grivas dies. Makarios attempts to regain control of government but flees to London in mid-July when a junta-ordered National Guard coup topples his administration. Pro-enosis forces jail or kill his supporters. On July 20, Turkey attacks Cyprus. In Greece the junta falls from power. Britain, Greece, and Turkey attend peace talks. On August 14, negotiations reach a deadlock, and Turkey launches the second phase of fighting. After gaining control of northern Cyprus, Turkey agrees to a UN cease-fire on August 16, and the Attila Line is established. President Makarios returns in December.

1975 Intercommunal negotiations begin. In February Turkish Cypriots, without declaring independence, proclaim northern Cyprus as the Turkish Federated State of Cyprus with Rauf Denktaş as president. Community leaders agree to a voluntary population exchange.

1977 Markarios and Denktaş agree that Cyprus should be a bizonal, bicommunal federation. Makarios dies in August. Spyros Kyprianou becomes president in southern Cyprus.

1983 In November Denktaş declares the independence of the Turkish Republic of Northern Cyprus (TRNC). Of the international community, only Turkey recognizes the TRNC.

1985 Talks collapse between Kyrpianou and Denktaş.

1988 George Vassiliou wins the presidency in the Republic of Cyprus. Vassiliou calls for Cyprus's demilitarization. Denktaş and Vassiliou resume UN-sponsored intercommunal talks in September.

1989 Vassiliou resists the Turkish Cypriot demand for self-determination. Denktaş objects to continuing talks without recognition of the TRNC. Tensions between communities increase as Greek Cypriot protesters violate the UN buffer zone and the TRNC arrests them.

1990 In July the Republic of Cyprus submits an application for European Community (EC) membership. Denktaş threatens not to resume intercommunal talks and to tighten ties with Turkey.

1992 Talks fail to progress due to Turkish Cypriot objections to a UN "set of ideas." In November the UN suggests implementing confidence-building measures (CBMs).

1993 Glafkos Clerides becomes president of the Republic of Cyprus. In November Greeks and Greek Cypriots agree to make joint decisions about a Cyprus settlement and to enter into a common defense pact.

1994 UN talks collapse in May when Denktaş rejects the CBMs as presented. The European Union (EU, formerly the EC) confirms that the Republic of Cyprus can become a member and rules that member-countries cannot import TRNC agricultural goods. The TRNC and Turkey form tighter bonds.

1996 An August motorcycle rally triggers violence along the Attila Line.

1997 The Republic of Cyprus orders a Russian anti-aircraft missile system, generating Turkish objections. Cypriot presidents meet for the time since 1994. Further talks are postponed until after the Republic of Cyprus presidential elections in February 1998.

SELECTED BIBLIOGRAPHY

Denktaş, R. R. *The Cyprus Triangle*, rev. ed. New York: Office of the Turkish Republic of Northern Cyprus, 1988.

Denktaş, Rauf R. *Letters of Cyprus*. Lefkoşa (Nicosia): Ministry of Foreign Affairs and Defence of the TRNC, 1996.

Durrell, Lawrence. *Bitter Lemons*. New York: Penguin Books, 1991.

Geography Department. *Cyprus in Pictures*. Minneapolis: Lerner Publications, 1992.

Geography Department. *Greece in Pictures*. Minneapolis: Lerner Publications, 1996.

Geography Department. *Turkey in Pictures*. Minneapolis: Lerner Publications, 1988.

International Affairs Agency. *Cyprus Reality.* Lefkoşa (Nicosia): International Affairs Agency of the TRNC, 1996.

Kelling, George. *Countdown to Rebellion.* New York: Greenwood Press, 1990.

Loizos, Peter. *The Heart Grown Bitter: A Chronicle of Cypriot War Refugees.* Cambridge: Cambridge University Press, 1981.

Ministry of Foreign Affairs. *Turkish Brutal Actions in Cyprus in August 1996 and Their Implications.* Nicosia: Republic of Cyprus Ministry of Foreign Affairs, 1996.

Necatigil, Zaim M. *The Cyprus Question and the Turkish Position in International Law,* 2d ed. Oxford: Oxford University Press, 1993.

Oberling, Pierre. *Double Representation Conspiracy: How the Greek and Greek Cypriot Governments Are Precipitating a New Crisis in Cyprus by Using the European Union.* Lefkoşa (Nicosia): Public Relations Department of the TRNC, 1997.

Oberling, Pierre. *Negotiating for Survival: The Turkish Cypriot Quest for a Solution to the Cyprus Problem.* Princeton: Aldington Press, 1991.

Oberling, Pierre. *Road to Bellapais: The Turkish Cypriot Exodus to Northern Cyprus.* (East European Monographs, No. 125.) Boulder, CO: Social Science Monographs, 1982.

Press and Information Office. *Cyprus.* Nicosia: Republic of Cyprus Press and Information Office, 1990.

Solsten, Eric, ed. *Cyprus: A Country Study,* 4th ed. Washington, D.C.: Federal Research Division, Library of Congress, 1993.

Vanezis, P. N. *Makarios: Pragmatism v. Idealism.* London: Abelard-Schuman, 1974.

INDEX

ABOUT THE AUTHOR

Tom Streissguth

Tom Streissguth has traveled widely in Europe and the Middle East. During the 1980s he lived in Greece, where he taught English as a second language. As a specialist in the areas of geography and European history, he has written numerous books, including *France, Japan, Mexico,* and *Russia* for Carolrhoda Books. He is the author of a book for young adults called *International Terrorists* (Oliver Press) and has written several biographies. Mr. Streissguth contributed to *Cyprus in Pictures* and *Greece in Pictures,* also published by Lerner Publications Company. When he's not writing books, Mr. Streissguth enjoys spending time with his wife and two daughters at their home in Florida.

ABOUT THE CONSULTANT

Andrew Bell-Fialkoff, *World in Conflict* series consultant, is a specialist on nationalism, ethnicity, and ethnic conflict. He is the author of *Ethnic Cleansing,* published by St. Martin's Press in 1996, and has written numerous articles for *Foreign Affairs* and other journals. He is currently writing a book on the role of migration in the history of the Eurasian Steppe. Mr. Bell-Fialkoff lives in Bradford, Massachusetts.

SOURCES OF QUOTED MATERIAL

p. 21 Tad Szulc, "Cyprus: A Time of Reckoning," *National Geographic* 184, no. 1 (July 1993): 120; p. 24 Reuters, "In Cyprus, Turkish Foreign Minister Defends Her Country's Flag, *New York Times,* 16 Aug. 1996, A5; p. 29 Pierre Oberling, *The Double Representation Conspiracy: How the Greek and Greek Cypriot Governments Are Precipitating a New Crisis in Cyprus by Using the European Union* (Lefkoşa [Nicosia]: Public Relations Department of the TRNC, 1997), 19; p. 29 Reuters, "In Cyprus, Turkish Foreign Minister Defends Her Country's Flag, *New York Times,* 16 Aug. 1996, A5; p. 33 Tumer Halil, "Cyprus Problem, The End of Cypriots?" *Crossings* 1, no. 1 (April 1996), Turgut Durduran's Cyprus website, http://www.stwing.upenn.edu/~durduran/cyprus1.html; p. 42 Pierre Oberling, *The Road to Bellapais: The Turkish Cypriot Exodus to Northern Cyprus,* East European Monographs, No. 125 (Boulder, CO: Social Science Monographs, 1982), 15; p. 45 Ibid, 52; p. 49 Eric Solsten, ed., *Cyprus: A Country Study,* 4th ed. (Washington, DC: Federal Research Division, Library of Congress, 1993), 29; p. 49 Ibid., 28; p. 50 Ibid.; p. 50 Pierre Oberling, *The Road to Bellapais: The Turkish Cypriot Exodus to Northern Cyprus,* East European Monographs, No. 125 (Boulder, CO: Social Science Monographs, 1982), 56; p. 52 Ibid., 59; p. 54 Ibid., 56; p. 55 Ibid, 68; p. 55 Ibid.; p. 57 *The Akritas Plan,* "B. The Internal Aspect," 4b. Full version published in Greek by S. Papageorghiou in *Ta Khirisima Dokumenta tou Kypriakou,* vol. A (Athens, 1983), 250–7. Quoted in Zaim M. Necatigil, *The Cyprus Question and the Turkish Position in International Law,* 2nd ed. (Oxford: Oxford University Press, 1993), 407; p. 70 Eric Solsten, ed., *Cyprus: A Country Study,* 4th ed. (Washington, DC: Federal Research Division, Library of Congress, 1993), 38; p. 70 Ibid.; p. 71 *London Times,* 3 July 1967, 5F. Quoted in Pierre Oberling, *The Road to Bellapais: The Turkish Cypriot Exodus to Northern Cyprus,* East European Monographs, No. 125 (Boulder, CO: Social Science Monographs, 1982), 136; p. 73 International, "Cyprus: The Guns of August," *Newsweek,* 2 Sept. 1974, 33; p. 77 International, "Uproar," *Newsweek,* 27 Dec. 1954, 29; p. 81 U.S. Department of State, *Department of State Bulletin* (Jan. 1984), vol. 84, no. 2082; p. 82 UN Secretary-General's report to the Security Council about the Cyprus situation, S/ 24830 (19 Nov. 1992), para. 63. Quoted in Zaim M. Necatigil, *The Cyprus Question and the Turkish Position in International Law,* 2nd ed. (Oxford: Oxford University Press, 1993), 397; p. 85 Europe, "Twitchy Turks," *Economist* 342, no. 7999 (11 Jan. 1997): 48; p. 86 Embassy of Cyprus Press and Information Office, "President Clerides Committed to Make Every Effort to Achieve Progress," *Cyprus Newsletter* (Washington, DC: Embassy of Cyprus, July 1997), 1; p. 87 Jean Christou, "Gap Between Sides in Cyprus Still Enormous," *Cyprus Mail.* Quoted in *Kypros-Net* on the Republic of Cyprus government website, http://www.kypros.org/News/Update/Talks_ July 97/071543.html; p. 97 *Our Island – Your Island* (Buntingford, England: Peace Child International, 1997), 58.